Energy Psychology /
Energy Medicine

The Practice of
Neuro-Kinesiology and
Psychoneuroimmunology
in Exploring the Mind/Body Connection

Art Martin N.D., Ph.D.
James Landrell D.C., H.M.D

Personal Transformation Press

Energy Psychology / Energy Medicine:
The Practice of Neuro Kinesiology and Psychoneuroimmunology
in Exploring the Mind/Body Commection
By Art Martin N.D., Ph.D. and James Landrell, D.C, H.M.D.

Copyright © 1990, 2004 Personal Transformation Press. All rights reserved.
9th Edition revised March 2005
Fourteeth printing March 2005

ISBN: 1-891962-07-8

Published by:
Personal Transformation Press
(A division of the Energy Medicine Institute
(a non-profit educational corporation)
8300 Rock Springs Road
Penryn, CA 95663
Phone: (916) 663-9178
Fax: (916) 663-0134
Orders only: (800) 655-3846
E-mail: artmartin@mindspring.com

Printed in the U.S.A.

Contents

Disclaimer

Please note the following statement:

We make *no claims* as to our abilities to heal or cure anyone of any dysfunction, illness or disease. We are not doctors, psychiatrists or any form of medical practitioners. We do not diagnose or prescribe any drugs.

Many people have described Psychoneuroimmunology and Neuro/Cellular Repatterning as Energy Medicine or Energy Psychology. We choose to describe it as "reprogramming the mind" since we view the body/mind as an electromagnetic biodynamic computer.

Even though we have experienced many miracles and healing results through the use of the modalities PNI and N/CR we are not the vehicle that performs the healing. Some of our results are miracles and may seem unreal and phenomenal at times, yet we are not healers. All healing is self healing. The power of the mind does the healing. All we are is software developers. Our software is affirmations. They must be installed by the individual that is seeking our help.

All we seek is the original base cause, core issue and the catalyst or activator that created the malfunctioning program. Our intent is to delete, erase, and clear the malfunctioning program or sub-personality and rewrite a new effective program that will support healing along with peace, happiness, harmony, joy, abundance and unconditional love and acceptance in an individuals life. In this manner we can detach from needs, wants and asking others to tell us we have value.

It is our intent to empower people so they can reclaim their personal power, rebuild their self-esteem, self-worth and self-confidence. In this way they can become self-validating individuals who can step onto their life path in peace, happiness, harmony and joy. All success is self-motivated. We can begin our spiritual journey as self-actualized people who have reclaimed their personal power and have no need to control, manipulate or have power or authority over anyone or anything.

To every person who has experienced physical, mental or emotional pain in any form:

Someday in the future, all practitioners, no matter what their specialty, will recognize that the body/mind is a hologram and must be addressed as a complete unit. For some reason, we have come to the basic understanding and conclusion that we can control pain and disease by suppressing the symptom with drugs, manipulating or removing the offending part of the body to heal it. What affects one part also has effects within the whole unit. Body, mind, and spirit interact to form an integrated, functioning entity. If you give yourself love, a feeling of alrightness and create a positive mental image, the body will heal itself through the power of the mind. The God Source, your Soul and teacher worked with you to create a perfect body, and included directions/lessons in the flight plan on how to have an abundant, happy, healthy life, yet you lost track of the flight plan and the directions. When you decided you knew more about the process of healing/recovery than your God-self, you separated from God and the inherent healing power through God-self to your mind. This is a world universal concept.

We dedicate this work to giving people a true understanding of the process of healing. Our mission is to give therapists, practitioners and their clients the opportunity to experience healing through love and forgiveness. It is our hope that people can understand that control, manipulation, judgment, authority, resentment and self-righteousness can only create rejection, anger and fear, which in turn causes pain, contraction and abandonment. This will eventually end up in dysfunctional behavior, depression, illness and disease. Love, forgiveness and acceptance cause happiness, expansion and healing. The mind's programming is the base cause of this discomfort.

With the knowledge offered here, people can make accurate choices to heal the fear that causes illness, disease, addiction, rage, uncontrolled anger, irrational behavior, dysfunctional relationships, fear of commitment and intimacy, mental and physical abnormalities without damage or pain to their body and mind. When we learn that there is no lack of love, we can heal our separation from ourselves and from God. We can heal anything with love and forgiveness. Recovery is possible and miracles do happen; all you must do is step out of illusion/denial and detach from needs and wants, so that you can take responsibility and tell the truth. Love, peace, happiness, joy, harmony are our entitlements and inheritance. We can have it all now.

Acknowledgments

It has been a rocky road since I was introduced to Paul Solomon and Ronald Beesley. Paul gave me the tools, guidance and the basic structure of spiritual psychology; Ronald gave me a basic understanding of the theory of hands-on healing and how the body interacts with its environment. Paul's teaching not only turned my life around, but it also gave me a career goal.

When I made a commitment not to go back to the business world, I found myself in unfamiliar surroundings, but I seemed to have a drive to find out what this was all about. These two teachers gave me an opportunity to connect the third dimensional reality with the esoteric. With this new knowledge, I was able to move from the unknown psychic/faith healing to an understandable and describable process that has duplicable results. I can explain healing in both scientific/medical terms and spiritual terminology.

When I first entered the healing field, I assumed that some people would get healed and others would not, with no explanation as to why. Solomon and Beasley opened my eyes as to why healing occurs. I am very appreciative and supportive of their work and the understanding that I received from them. I have since gone further and created my own theories and process. They provided the foundation, and the knowledge I gained from them was priceless. I thank them for becoming a part of my life.

At the Solomon workshops, I met Joshua Stone. He became a close friend and encouraged me to further my education and get a Master's degree in Psychology. I appreciate his support and help for me and my family during the transition years in the beginning of my research on my search for healing.

If it had not been for my clients who let me practice on them in the early years, Neuro/Cellular Repatterning would never have happened. I thank all who trained me and supported my practice, lectures and seminars. I have learned more from my work than I ever learned in a classroom.

I also want to thank all the people who supported me in presenting lectures and workshops. Jim Ingram and Pattie Marshall were pivotal in getting me to see my value and helping me present my experience. Chris Issel was the first person to ask if I could teach my healing process in 1987. Her confidence in me pushed me to new heights. Many other people sponsored workshops and I thank all of them for their support. Mike Hammer worked with me in 1989 to help present workshops. I appreciate his confidence in my work. He has since gone on in his own path in his destiny.

In 1991, I met Dr. John Craig. He turned my life upside down by demonstrating to me that we really never get all the blocks out of our reality. It is a lifetime experience. He spurred me on to new theories and got me started on this new path of being a spiritual being in a physical body.

Last but not least, I thank my sponsors over the years—Helen Phelps, Lesley Gregory, Joy Johnson, Oshara Miller, Julienne Stone, Arraya Lawrence, Betts Richter, Nancy Worthington, Illeneen Botting, Amy Kinder, Rob Pearla, Joyce Techel, Barbara Stone, Arlean Gotlieb, Ruth Johnson, Patricia Heavanston, Sache Nakono, Kitty Kartiala, Joan Noel, Dave Winter, Morningstar Black, Kate Moyer, Mindy Cantor, Steve Kaplan, Sally Machutta, Coral Loy, Pete Myronyk, David Schultz, Doni Schemm, and again, Jim Ingram and many more. I have had many sponsors in the last 20 years and I appreciate all the help I have received from them. Ken Peterson took what I had to offer and ran with it. He has worked with me for the past fourteen years and continues to work with me today. He is an inspiration to me, to this day.

I want to thank my wife, Susie, and my sons, Ross and Ryan, for their acceptance and riding the rocky road to transformation. I know we are now entering the period of abundance for all of us now.

People are finding the path that I have trod for the last 20 years has finally reaped its goal. Healing is totally explainable and we can heal anything if we will listen to the body/mind and reprogram the dysfunctional programs.

Preface

(from Fifth Edition 1995 printing)

I decided to include the 1995 preface to show where we were and the progress we have made in the last ten years. When I achieved clarity of purpose, new information came pouring in that changed the face of N/CR so much that many people who had taken workshops in the past claimed they almost had to learn the process all over again. We added so much more in the following years that changed the face of N/CR to the point where we had revise this manual each time to bring it up to the current level of practice.

There is a time in people's lives when they will let go and give up control, authority, and self-righteousness in their life so that they recognize what service is. Very few people listen to themselves or the world around or beyond them. When we let go of the need to control, exert authority, manipulate others, be the victim of others' behavior and make peace with our Middle Selves and our inner selves, we can receive the messages that are coming to us. Most of the time we have become too attached to outcomes and are too busy making a living or impressing other people to really live our life. In many cases, it is pure survival. The dialogue we have with our body goes on, but we do not listen.

Few people know that there is a Higher Source of their being that would like to talk to us and give guidance. It seems as if most of us shut ourselves off from the outside world, locked up in the inner struggle to make a living. This all changed for me in 1978, when I sold my restaurant with a driving desire to find out who I was and why I am here.

This manual is a result of 25 years of research, working with over 20 healing processes. In my search, the goal was to develop a program that would encompass what I considered to be the most effective parts of various healing processes. In developing N/CR, I viewed all programs in an eclectic manner. I would try them all. If they worked with my challenges and if they proved to be workable over time and showed pragmatic results, they became a part of Neuro/Cellular Repatterning. As a result, N/CR became a format which could be integrated into most healing processes. Every process or exercise that has become a part of this manual for the training has been proven and documented over the last 15 years. For documentation, read the case histories in chapter 17 of *Your Body is Talking: Are You Listening?*

A considerable amount of the material about the process in this manual can be unbelievable and confrontational to those who are locked into the medical model with their doubter and skeptical sub-personalities active. We have been confronted by skeptics who doubted that we could accomplish the results we claimed. Of course, we make no claims or guarantee that this will work with everyone, as it is *individuals* who heal themselves. We are only facilitators who can reprogram the mind. When we discovered that the mind/body was an electromagnetic biodynamic computer, this opened the door to the miracles that have resulted from the process of Neuro/Cellular Repatterning.

When we began this process of discovery in 1978, I did not know where I was going. I had one goal in mind—to find a way to eliminate my pain that began in 1954. In 1978, I found Paul Solomon and Ronald Beesley, and began the road to healing. When I discovered that the mind controlled all functions of the body, this was the final piece that would eventually be the basic form of Neuro/Cellular Repatterning. My discovery that affirmations were the software for the mind created the format for N/CR. Until 1986, I used four affirmations, but when I met Elaine, a Science of Mind Minister, she suggested that I let my mind construct the affirmations as it could tap into the situation and create the most appropriate affirmation. I was willing to try and it worked. This opened up a new concept in healing. As we progressed, the affirmations expanded until I found that I could form an affirmation to meet any situation that was presented.

In 1987, I was approached by Chris Issel about teaching the process. I wrote up three pages that we used for our guidelines. We set up an eight-week schedule, meeting one night a week. Eight people attended the workshop, which began teaching the process that I described as Structural Body/Mind Balancing.

1n 1987, it expanded more when Jim Ingram suggested we might be able to teach this to more people by giving lectures and workshops. In 1989, Mike Hammer expanded the scope more as he joined me in presenting workshops. That year, we changed the name to Neuro/Cellular Repatterning. An eight-page handout described the work and some of the affirmations. At that time, we could teach the whole process in a one-day workshop.

It expanded more in 1990 when Jim Landrell, a chiropractor who was very interested in the work, helped expand the concepts into a two-day workshop and a new manual with more information. We had a few affirmations and no body map to guide us. We now have this manual today and what I consider a very effective process that will heal any dysfunction … if the client is committed. Many of my clients tell me, "I do not understand how to take responsibility for my life." We have just recently found some of the reasons for this and I am sure we will find more in the future, but I have no idea when that will be.

Seldom is the outward manifestation the base cause. To be a therapist takes a considerable clarity. Just having a degree and/or some acceptance in a field of therapy does not guarantee effectiveness. To be an effective therapist, you must be in recovery yourself. There are many therapists who assume they "have the knowledge" and forget that they must work regularly on their own recovery with another therapist. I have found that very few therapists are actually pursuing recovery in their own life. We all get into healing work to find ourselves, but very few are dealing with their own issues.

To practice N/CR takes detachment from control, judgment, and expectation, plus self-worth and self-confidence in order to handle the treatment process effectively. I became aware that healing is entirely up to the client. We can suppress or cause a dysfunction to go into remission, but is that a cure? In my research, I discovered that you could not heal anything unless the client had made the decision to heal at the Subconscious level. It is up to clients to decide if they want to make that commitment; once that commitment is there, anything can be healed with love and forgiveness.

Many of the miracles in the past 15 years always seemed to happen when the clients were "at the end of their rope" and made a commitment to change. At this point, it seems that anything is possible. We have seen bones, vertebrae, and discs reform. We have not found any dysfunction of the body or mind for which we cannot locate base cause. We tend not to describe disease by names, because they are all the same—lack of love. Our biggest problem is to get the ego to see that its programs are not serving the body well. If we can get that across, and the person has made the commitment to be healed, a miracle can happen. It could be spontaneous or take hours, weeks or months. People have asked me, "Why does it seem that no matter what *you* do, nothing happens, although others have experienced miracles in their life?" Some would get angry at me, or at God, for withholding the miracles. But we have no control over the results nor the effectiveness of the work since it is all self-healing. Only the individual has total control over the results.

My intention in developing N/CR was to give the practitioner a set of tools that could, if used properly, heal any dysfunction, from the mental programming that seems to have no viable cause, to emotional codependency, addictive relationships, physical breakdown in the body, life-threatening diseases, to physical and genetic dysfunctions. It is very easy to release physical pain because it reveals itself, but emotional or mental disorders are much harder, since they are non-tangible.

However, so far, we have not been stumped by any dysfunction. We can always get to the base cause and the core issue, but causing healing to take place will not happen unless the client displays commitment. In the early years, we focused on ego as being the enemy with an agenda to control our life. In the first issue of this manual, we mercilessly beat up ego as the villain and enemy. "We are not exactly sure who is the problem but we know it is in the mind." You can see this by some of the affirmations in the back of manual.

When we start to participate in true healing, we find that clients unwilling to take responsibility for their own healing will find every excuse to avoid being healed. Most of the time, it's the practitioner's fault; it makes no difference what the excuse is—any will do. That is a mind's trap—justification, excuses, and self-righteousness; it works every time when clients do not want to see their path clearly. Placing your self-worth on the line with a client who has no commitment to healing can be very discouraging and frustrating. I have found that detachment is very important. We must become compassionately detached. We can understand our clients' dilemmas, but we do not have to rescue or save them from themselves.

My second purpose is to offer a healing process to the world that I feel will be the true healing process of the future. Many people are talking about Cellular Memory, but I have found very few who are able to release it. Recent years have seen considerable discussion about Psychoneuroimmunology and what it can do for people, but few understand how to achieve sustainable results in their work. In N/CR, we are restructuring the cell structure by releasing the dysfunctional programming that is causing genetic defects or cellular degeneration. We have seen the results of healing pragmatically. It has been verified and checked over the years for relapses. We have done many double-blind studies and tests to verify N/CR. The results have had a success rate of over 95%.

Arthur H. Martin
September 1995

Preface to the Ninth Edition

This is the ninth revision since 1995. In this description, you will find that we have come a long way since we started to develop N/CR in 1979. In 1999, we discovered that we were practicing the basic concepts of Psychoneuroimmunology, which gives us scientific backing to the work now. We were aware that brain chemicals such as neuropeptides were the carriers of information in the body, but we were not sure how they performed their task. Our research discovered cellular memory and that if it was released, a person's attitude and behavior would change, many times creating permanent healing on the spot. PNI has opened new vistas for us now that show us an understanding of how the body communicates through the receptor sites in every organ and gland in the body. They control all cellular function in all areas of the body.

Positive mind set and positive mental image (PMI) are no longer just clichés. Since we know how it is created, we can lock PMI in. Preventing clients from sinking into negative reactions takes considerable monitoring. Negative reactions cause immediate suppression of the immune and endocrine systems, and then work outward causing breakdowns in all organs and glands. With the immune system in suppression, it is open season for any infection to take hold, and further degeneration can cause major breakdowns in body function.

We have crossed many bridges since the original manual for Neuro/Cellular Repatterning was written in 1987. The last revision was September, 2001. Each revision has always brought about new challenges. I decided to leave the 1991 preface in the manual and bring it up to the 1995 edition because it gives an insight to where we were at that time. At that time, I was really getting into the recovery process. I had attended many AA, ACA and CoDA conferences because I wanted to understand how the 12-Step recovery movement was approaching the therapy/ recovery program. With John Bradshaw *et al* coming to the forefront, my work was easier because I no longer had to explain the dysfunctional family syndrome. My training was in the format with Fritz Perles top dog/underdog, Virginia Satir and Carl Roger family systems theory. The recovery movement was bringing the theory and concept down to a more acceptable, understandable dialogue.

You will notice in this manual we have taken a new and revised view of how the mind operates. We no longer see ego as the enemy and demon of the mind that has an agenda to control and destroy our life. We now see it as an ally, with which we must make friends and work with. My very shallow understanding of Middle Self has expanded as we discovered what its role was and how it worked within the mind. We found out who they are and how they interact with us in our life. We discovered ego is not the enemy at all. In fact, it is our friend. It is the retriever for our memory and secretary for the Subconscious Mind. When I stopped beating it up, my memory improved almost miraculously.

We found that Middle Self was not the enemy either, but was our protector that tried to keep our life on the straight and narrow, like a rudder that helps us run our life when we walk out. We found the sub-personalities that were created were the true enemies. By not being in our power, they took over, directed by the personality's selves. So in a sense we are at blame because we did not take control over our life and gave our power away.

As children, it was very hard to understand that we were in control, as the adults and our primary caregivers seemed to be in control. Very seldom do adults realize that they are setting up a child to fail if they set up negative input. Middle Self did the best it could with the programs it had available to work with to protect us and provide security and safety. When we do not take control over our life, it is run by a committee that seems to have no director, so some programs run amuck such as serious diseases.

In the last few years, we became aware that the Magical Child syndrome was operating in 95 out of 100 of our clients. We also discovered that Artificial Intelligence was created in the Conscious Mind to take over the task of running our lives when we walked out. My discovery that Conscious Mind would split into three separate operating systems during a traumatic experience added more complication. When it splits apart due to traumatic experiences, we walk out and Inner Child enters the picture, creating Magical Child to operate from. Our mind is a very complex computer, operating from four basic operating systems. When we lose control by walking out into Magical Child, each operating system is set up with back-up systems to run our life, but they may not run our life the way we would choose. If we are not present, then somebody has to be driving our vehicle. We developed this process as we went along finding different aspects as clients presented their specific situation to us.

In the last 25 years, I have experienced many different processes and treatments that were *supposed* to release pain and reprogram the body/mind, yet that was not my experience. The symptoms always seemed to come back. People could not seem to get on target in their life and accomplish their goals.

To this date, I have met only two people who were doing work that would release pain immediately and permanently. When you are dealing with a non-tangible such as anger or fear, many people can make claims, but does it work in the long term? The only way we will know for sure is the test of time. N/CR has met the test of time. We have clients who have been through a few years to 20 years with no recurring symptoms. Diseases and genetic defects that were released have never recurred. If another catalyst or crisis comes up, does the person handle the situation in a detached, unattached manner? Or do they fall back into the old pattern? This question must be asked and tracking has to be done to verify the pragmatic results.

When I published *Becoming A Spiritual Being In A Physical Body*, this became one of the major steps in my theory about how to get where we want to be. It is a reading assignment for this course of study.

In 1996, with the invention of the Harmonizer, now renamed the StressBuster, we entered a new frontier in the work, now that we can protect ourselves from stress from outside elements. It also will realign the body's electromagnetic field and interact with the neurological system, bringing our immune and endocrine systems up to 100% function in about 10 days to two weeks. It also has many other uses as described in the Appendix.

When we realized that we were practicing the basic concepts of and achieving the results described in Psychoneuroimmunology, we knew we had the answers to the healing modality of the future. Some of the material may be confronting and seem far out but it is all been proven over the last 29 years to work extremely well.

With all the new discoveries in the last four years, this manual has been completely rewritten to bring it up to current practice. We have now expanded to a series of workshops as the material has increased fourfold since 1992. This has always and will always be a work-in-progress, as we work our way through the jungle of our mind and the amazing awesome abilities it possesses to both destroy our life and heal our life if we will listen to the lessons it presents to us each. You can scale the highest mountain but you need a good map to reach your goal. Your mind can provide all the directions and maps to the path to success and abundance in every task you choose to master.

Happy sailing into the new frontier of healing with Behavioral Mind Body Medicine.

With love,
Art Martin
March 2005 Penryn, CA

Chapter 1

An Introduction to Understanding the Human Condition

Everyone would like to be successful and reach a level in their life where they have abundance at every level. The attitude and concept that governs our ability to set our goals and attain them is the level at which we can conceive what success is. To many, just having roof to live under, enough food on the table and a TV to watch would be success. It depends on how well we are able to see beyond the blinders and limitations we put on our selves that governs our level of success, on how far we can see past our limitations that control our ability to achieve our goals.

Sometimes we get lost in our vision and passion because we receive validation for how we are performing, and we see that as the level of success we can attain. So, we miss the higher goal because we are getting so much support where we are. We do not know there is another level because our blinders block our view so we never reach for the higher goal. Throughout my life, I have confronted the challenges that came before me and overcome them. If someone challenged me by saying I could not do something, I would go after it and succeed. Each step opened a new door, yet I was unable to see the level of unlimited opportunities until I had walked this path for twenty years.

The question is: Can we recognize our illusion? If we are living inside our illusion there is no possible way we can step out it. How are we going to step out of illusion and face the issues that confront us if we can't see them? The first task we have is to recognize there is a challenge before us. I have found that most people do not even recognize there is something malfunctioning in their life. How do we get around the illusion and denial created by Conscious Rational Mind? It created autopilot and artificial intelligence to run our life. Most of us function out of the past imprinting we received from our parents; as a result we are not able to see a true picture. It really does not make any difference where you are in your life path as far as the category you fit into. You can be from an extremely wealthy family and have the same problems as a person from a poor family living in the ghetto. The key factor is, was your family a functional or dysfunctional family. Children from functional families have a much better chance of success. A constructive family model and strong family values will teach a child trust, respect, personal value, self-esteem, self-worth and self-confidence. If the parents do not have these values themselves, they cannot model or teach them to their children. Parents can only teach and model at their level of competence that was passed on to them by their parental imprinting.

Contrary to popular belief, there are those children who succeed against all odds. Who are they and how do they fit in to the bell curve rating on the scale below? It takes drive, intention, commitment, discipline, and the ability to follow through to a goal. Some people have the drive no matter what family circumstances or under what conditions they were born into.

There is another factor to deal with, too. If the negative programming is not dealt with somewhere during our life, we melt down when the lessons come up. We can't will ourselves through life. Even extremely successful people can fall out if they do not deal with personal development some time during their life. This is why we see very successful people dying at a young age. The stress of the lessons caught up with them. They may be nice, supportive, generous people but the lesson of self-acceptance, self-value, and self-validation was eating them up internally and will produce a life-threatening disease or a total melt down where they are rendered dysfunctional in their life so they can do nothing, to the point someone has to take care of them.

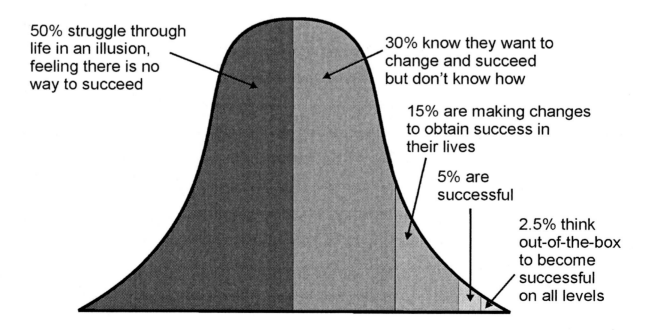

50% struggle through life in an illusion, feeling there is no way to succeed

30% know they want to change and succeed but don't know how

15% are making changes to obtain success in their lives

5% are successful

2.5% think out-of-the-box to become successful on all levels

Most people resist being categorized, yet we place ourselves in these groups based on the behavior we exhibit to the world around us. Our internal message we send out on a nonverbal level, known as meta-communication, reaches our intended audience before we open our mouth.

It does not make any difference what group you are in, from the high level wealthy to the lower financial class, everybody seems to fit into the 60-20-15-5 rule. Even though the successful group may have the financial business success strategy down, most of them ignore their mental, psychological, physical and spiritual health. The average person does not realize that all four quadrants of health must addressed to attain perfect health. We know most people in the lower classes have problems with sickness and emotional conflicts due to their lack of knowledge of proper diet, nutrition and exercise. Plus their inability to deal emotional conflicts adds up to an instable life style. We would assume that the more educated you are, the more attention you would pay to diet, nutritional needs, mental/emotional and spiritual health, but less than one third of the population pay any attention to these needs. This is why you see people with disabilities, life threatening illnesses and dying at young ages when they seem to have it all together.

There are only four types of people in every grouping:
- The bulk of the population at 60% does not see any way out of their dilemma. They do not complain and trudge on each day.
- Victims make up 30%. They see everybody doing it to them or nobody willing to help them.
- Survivors at 15% are making an attempt to change their life but most cannot recognize the illusion they are in until they apply themselves. When they do they can usually step in the successful group
- Winners – only 5% – have it their way and will not change, yet only half of these people out-of-the-box thinkers.

Which category do you fit into? 40% have a chance to create a successful life yet only about 15% of them actually find some form of success. You have to be on the right side of the Bell Curve to make changes in your life. If you are at the top of the curve you may be able slide down the right side but it take awareness and committed intention to achieve the goal of success. The winners are all clustered at the lower right side of the curve. In fact only 50% of the winners are 'out-of-the-box' thinkers. Even though they may control all the money in the world, many are not happy nor successful in their personal lives. We all have the opportunity to become winners if we can find the path to personal transformation and our millionaire mind. Success and happiness are relative terms. It depends on your level of awareness as to where you believe your happiness is. To a person on the left side of the Bell Curve who accepts that an occasional weekend in the park with their children and two weeks vacation a year may be happy in his/her world. To an out-of-the-box thinker, that would be like having no freedom. Then we have to ask what is freedom and how do you define it. It all depends on what your viewpoint of freedom is. To an out-of-the-box thinker, it's about being free to do what you desire to do at whatever time you decide to do it, without concern as to how much it will cost you. (In Chapter 10, we go through the mental/psychological attitude evaluation that will define your level of freedom and out-of-the-box thinking.)

Many talk about wanting to make changes in their life, but never embark on the journey or even step on the path. Fear of the unknown and change will cause people to cling to the known even if it creates pain and suffering. When they are in the pain they cannot see beyond the illusion they set up to block themselves from the truth. If they can perceive what they are doing to themselves with pain, illness and disease, they could release it immediately.

There is a "Catch-22" here, too. We must first recognize that we are in the compromising position we put ourselves in, which denies us the ability to get to the goal we say we want. I find that 90% do not recognize their self-imposed limitations and the blinders they have, due to ignorance or assuming that everything is all right in their life the way it is.

Are you going to go for it and fully participate in taking control of your life? You must let go of all blame, anger and resentment. To pull out of the downward spiral, you must be willing to forgive anyone and everyone who participated in your trauma, downfall or adversity. We find that only about 20% of the people who have attended our events have made that commitment, and less than 35% of that original 20% will follow through to get their life on the fast track and become a winner.

The question you must ask is: "Where am I on my path to recovery?" Most people focus on money and wealth, thinking that will buy them freedom and happiness. However, it will not meet any of our inner needs. When we move from needs and wants to knowingness we have crested the hill to success and happiness. You never have to question if you are on the right path as everything always manifests perfectly even though you may not believe at first. Peace, happiness, harmony, joy, perfect health, unconditional love, acceptance and abundance come when we reach the goal in our recovery where all the roadblocks to total wellness are overcome. When boulders come up in the path, we just push them out of way and say, "Next."

When I was afraid to finish a project for fear that I would not do it right, my friends were observing in me my past experience. The mountain I had to scale was that my father would not accept or approve what I had accomplished. Even after my father passed on, breaking that barrier was still a challenge. For years after his death, I continued laboring under the illusion that he was still looking over my shoulder at whatever I did. Inner validation was a complex, tough mountain for me to climb, and attaining it took me 15 years after my father died.

The reason I keep pushing forward and pulling the blinders back was that I knew success was more than accomplishing a task. The situation that confronted me was, the more I strived for a higher level of success, the more friends began to drop out of my life. We no longer had common experiences to talk about. I was getting too far out for them to deal with me. As I went forward on my goal to find a methodology to heal my pain and limitations, I was always feeling that I was not accepted by people who I desired to be friends with. It was a lonely path for many years but I knew that I would emerge from the tunnel to find a new reality.

The new reality did not come until I recognized that I was projecting out an incongruent message. I consciously believed people should accept me now that I'd changed my belief of who I was. Internally I had not changed the belief even though I thought I had. The "I am not accepted" belief was still projecting out due to the fact I needed outer validation and I was not getting it. To some people, I appeared self-righteous because I was always trying to justify who I was. I was sabotaging myself, yet I could not see the illusion. By working with people I had trained, I was able to release this image. When I realized this was happening, my internal message shifted.

We have lived our vision for 25 years. Now it is time to remove all the limitations and aspire to unlimited success, which we are doing now. Bridging the gap has been a real challenge. I decided, 18 months ago, to pull all the stops no matter what the cost. I would go all out to see if I could move into the world of marketing success. We are on the way to accomplishing our goals now. Without the knowledge I gained from my research over the last 25 years, I would never have broken the barriers that hold us back from success. My formula for success is contained in this manual.

I accept that the success formula provides an ability to do what you desire when you choose to do it, without any limitations or concern about how you are going to accomplish your desire or goal. Now that we have cracked the mind's codes, everything is possible. We have located all the files that control our mind. We have all the keys to how the mind processes information and files it in the Subconscious Mind's database. Our Subconscious Mind is the key to the future of abundance, joy and happiness.

The question is: "Can you tap into that vast data base of information?" Even though we have the tools to tap this reservoir of knowledge, fewer than 5% of the people know about it and less 20% of those will follow through to change their life path. Our mind is a complex set of operating systems we must master to become the computer programmer. When we get to the level where we can open the data base it will reveal to us every aspect of our life. Very few of us have even a smattering of knowledge what is blocking us from unlimited success.

Psychoneuroimmunology was the result of the practice of Energy Psychology and Energy Medicine. We had described N/CR as a somatic psychotherapy process, yet we have found it encompasses many formats. We can track any dysfunction, situation or malfunction in a person's life and locate the exact age or date when that conflict happened. Sometimes we can track it down to the exact hour, who participated and what was said that caused the misinterpretation or belief that created a dysfunctional program.

When I started developing this process, it was a very effective modality at the time. Little did I know that over the next 20 years, it would progress to where it is now. It seemed as if I was the laboratory and researcher. If I could clear the issue or program from myself, we would find a client who had the same situation or condition. My challenge to people who attended my seminars, lectures or read my books was, "You present or name the condition and we will find the root cause and the core issue." The more we found, the broader our scope became. We have found that there is no form of affliction, dysfunction or condition that can stop us. We can locate the cause of any illness, disease, behavioral dysfunction or condition that blocks or limits a person from attaining total and complete wellness, peace, happiness, harmony, joy, unconditional love and financial abundance.

If you do not deal with the programs locked in your mind from past lives and childhood experiences, they will eventually win you over and crash your life. We are entitled to peace, happiness, harmony, joy, unconditional love, acceptance and abundance.

We assumed that healing was a mechanical process. If you release the cellular memory and/or the beliefs, the pain or the cause will be released because release signals to the mind that the program is deleted. We have discovered that this does not always work because programs that are locked into the mind may be in different locations. We may get the surface location, which will release the immediate situation, but it also can be hidden in denial or denial of denial. Or Middle Self can create activator viruses similar to computer viruses that can activate with a crisis situation, statement, or an interplay from sensory input. When they activate, they create the whole program over again, which will install all the same files that we had assumed we'd released. It was very disappointing to find the program come back when you thought it was cleared.

Most alternative healing processes will clear up situations and pain, etc., but I have found that most of them work only on symptoms, not the cause. Some claim to be working on the cause but few can pragmatically document the results. Some can point to a few miracles, but is it across the board?

Placebo healing takes place all the time—it is not the therapist who heals anyone, but the individual who heals himself. If the client believes in your process and knows it will work, it will work … and you have a miracle. But, does that mean you accomplished it? N/CR has been through double blind test studies and emerged with flying colors when we discovered that therapy work is like peeling an onion. One layer leads to another layer. It is not a quick fix or a one-time hit, but a matter of releasing the layers as they come up. Many times our mind will lock in layers in many locations in various operating systems in our mind and they will not be revealed until we clear each layer and get down to the base cause or core issue. If we have a lesson that our mind senses we must learn, it will not release illness, disease or pain until we recognize and release the lesson. When we come to full awareness of the lesson, release, and love and forgive ourselves, the pain will be released.

As the pressure from the speeding up of time and the level of psychic intensity increase, many people are freaking out. As the pressure builds, we will see more senseless killing, murder-suicides and a rampant increase in death from disease. This indicates a need to be clear with your purpose and to release all of the emotional garbage that could cause you to lose your center. The more we get on purpose and become unattached to what *should be*, the more we can live in the now moment. Releasing illusion and denial are paramount. You can only see what you believe, which put us into a Catch-22 if you feel you must see it to believe it. This will keep you in denial of denial, spinning with no direction.

When we understand the power our Subconscious Mind has to disable our immune system, we will recognize how disease is created. If you analyze the Subconscious Mind as a computer, you will see that it can only do the tasks that have been programmed into it. If you have false beliefs or are living in denial of these beliefs, then you have no control over the computer.

In computer terms, the body and mind are the hardware. The software is the programs that are installed in the mind. The Instinctual Mind is just that; if you go into survival, it takes over. It has no ability to reason, process, or make rational decisions. The Conscious Mind is the programmer, and can also hold false beliefs and concepts you are not aware of. If you do not question these beliefs, they will run your life. The Conscious Mind must be on track all the time. If you walk out and go on autopilot, the Middle Self and the Subconscious Mind will take over, because somebody has to be at the wheel.

N/CR is an eclectic process that came from my desire to find a process that would actually cause healing to take place during client sessions. I was not satisfied with releasing pain or emotions in a cathartic release, only to have them return a few days later. Often, we feel we have actually released the problem, but, in my experience, if you give the practitioner authority, you will do almost anything he wants you to do. For example, all hypnosis is self-hypnosis and is self-induced. You must give the therapist permission to do what he is doing with you. In fact, we are being hypnotized all the time by TV, radio, magazines, newspapers, or anyone in authority. When we let what we read, hear or receive in our Conscious and Subconscious Minds program us and create our belief system, the challenge is to dehypnotize people so they awaken and take responsibility for their lives.

We are not aware of all the sensory input that results in programming in our mind. The Subconscious Mind is awake 24 hours day and can operate up to ten tracks if it needs to pick information. It will run that information through your files to see if there is any program about how you handled the situation in the past. If not, it will create a response without your knowledge. So the challenge is not how to hypnotize people to access information, but how to dehypnotize people so they can take responsibility and claim their personal power.

N/CR can do that, but there is a catch—practitioners cannot do it for clients; they must do it for themselves. If they are encased in illusion, they will not see the possibility. I have had clients ask, "How did that person heal himself? What did he do that I am not doing?" This question is almost unfathomable to the person who is in denial. It is very simple: When a person *desires* to change, he *decides* to claim his personal power and take responsibility in life. We cannot teach this desire/ decision process, nor can we cause a person to do it.

Seekers, doers and winners have many common traits that push them through transformation of their lives. In my research, I have found that these people do not give up. They seem to push forward with a desire to attain the goal they set out for themselves. The very successful people have a burning desire, coupled with an intense drive. There is a catch in this, too. Some of these people are workaholics with a need for validation that drives them. In time, they will burn out and melt down.

We must realize that it all can be very easy and without stress when we begin to accomplish our goals for ourselves because we have chosen to do it for ourselves. To do this, we must have the desire to accomplish the task.

1. When we do this we can set up a goal to attain and set out on the path.
2. Then we must stay on the path, by setting an intention as to how we are going to get to the goal.
3. Once we do this, we must use our determination and make a commitment to follow through.
4. To get to the goal, we must discipline ourselves to follow the path to our goal.
5. When we follow a consistent path, we will develop the habits to success.
6. When we accomplish the goal, we can set up a win-win attitude that will support us in the future.

Goal-setting can be very self-defeating and backfire on us if we just go through life, setting goals and never achieving them. We must be very specific about what the goals mean to us and whether they are near-term or long-term goals. Some goals can be set out to catch if the right situation comes up.

Chapter 2
The History of
Energy Psychology / Energy Medicine

Neuro/Cellular Repatterning (N/CR)™ is a new field of practice within Energy Psychology and Energy Medicine that uses love and forgiveness as the basic modalities—the only two modalities that will cause healing. N/CR will be one of the healing modalities of the future because it holds the promise of healing any dysfunction, emotional/mental problem, illness, or disease without pain, drugs or surgery. All diseases, illness, emotional or physical breakdowns are dysfunctional behavior patterns, but we don't need to know what the dysfunction is, nor must we name it or diagnose it. All we need to know is, what created it, and then we release it. By accepting the situation or the person who created the fear, rejection or anger, we release it with unconditional love and forgiveness. I finally found the solution with this new awareness. The delusion, denial and inability to take responsibility for our life are the blocks to total healing.

We have experienced miracles with hundreds of people. Spontaneous releases, in minutes, of any disease, emotional dysfunctions or genetic defects were amazing us. Yet some clients did not respond very well and the dysfunction would return. At this point, we realized that *we* were not doing it; we were not "healers" or therapists. We are only here to teach people how to love themselves and receive love. If you can make that shift in consciousness, permanent healing will result. We cannot change the holographic image that clients hold about themselves; we can only help them make the spiritual shift causing the healing. If they cannot shift, then the healing process will give them a temporary release.

We have found that N/CR will work in spite of clients because we are not working with the Conscious Mind. As a result we are able to duplicate the process with different people 95% of the time.

Since we are the script writer, producer and director of all the shows in our life, we ask Middle Self to let clients come out from the wings and take center stage. Now that they are the lead in their play, it will cooperate with them. This is accomplished by talking to the Middle Self with an affirmation and making peace with it. We let it know that it is an important part of the team and the client does not want to take its power away or destroy it.

It is not the modality that causes healing to happen, since many allopathic and alternative therapies have claimed provable visible healings, but they cannot explain why remission happens or how to reduplicate the process with any regularity. I have discovered that the key is the effectiveness of the practitioner to get in touch with clients' feeling self. You must set up a trust so the client feels that you care and love them—this is what allows healing to take place. Healing is governed by only one law—the law of LOVE, and it works every time. My study with *A Course in Miracles* formed part of the base. This is also documented in Dolores Kregar's book, *The Healing Touch.*

We now understand how the process works and we can explain it in scientific terms. Psychiatrists, doctors, psychologists, practitioners and lecturers have recognized the need to release negative emotions, yet few have accessed a controlled process which will get to the core issue. For more than five years, we were unable to accurately describe how N/CR worked, and had to come up with an acceptable scientific explanation for people in the medical field who were attending our workshops.

The results have shown that each practitioner achieves virtually the same results. Fear appears on the left side; anger on the right side of the body. All rejection deposits along the spine, and we found sixty individual locations for other specific emotional dysfunctional programs. So many doctors and medical researchers were giving us the answers to the puzzle of healing that it will take time to decipher them. A 1993 article in *Discovery Magazine*, "A Bug in The System" claimed that scientists had discovered the causes of disease syndrome, but they had no cure, prognosis, or way to correct it. They have labeled it a "genetic defect."

In fact, cellular breakdown is caused by the cell's mitochondria losing its ability to process and absorb nutrients. The cellular structure begins to collapse from lack of food, and begins to malfunction. Their interpretation is the cells are dying and will cause whatever diagnosis they hang on it. This fills in the missing link in understanding why healing works with N/CR. We erase the cellular memory of rejection, lack of love, etc., and we help the cell to recover its original blueprint. Then it begins to rebuild new healthy cells.

With counseling, physical therapy and most all alternative therapies, you can remove the energy that is causing the pain or discomfort. But, if you do not locate the root cause, healing will be a simple symptomatic release. We have just masked the problem until the same catalyst or stimulus reappears and causes the energy to build up again, reactivating the disease or dysfunctional emotional program. With N/CR we locate the core issue uncovering the Subconscious Mind's program. When an experience is filed, it creates a record and program with energy that makes small chemical changes in the body. Each program records how we reacted and handled the incident the first time. Each time we encounter this situation in the future, we build more patterns with instructions on how we will handle similar situations again. Eventually these chemical changes will cause a physical breakdown in the body. (This explained why my body was breaking down; conventional methods could not get to the base cause or the core issue.)

To release the dysfunctional emotion and the program, we must understand the cause and the reason you reacted the way you did. Now that we understand the dialogue your Subconscious Mind is having with your body, we can release it. When we have accomplished that, we then can erase the program's instructions, destroy the patterns and file the record, pattern and program in the history section of Subconscious Mind's archives. At this point, the energy is released and the behavior program is no longer accessible to you. Of course, if you are getting a lot of mileage out of the soap opera, you can create a new one.

At the physical level, the cellular memory is released, which allows the muscle to return to its original form. The short circuit in the meridian that caused the muscle to go into contraction from the emotional trauma is released. At the same the time, the patterns, the neuro-pathway created from the emotional experience, are released and erased. The original program for the muscles now takes over again and the pain is gone. In the case of a life threatening dysfunctional program, the same process happens. The endocrine system has its original programs restored so the immune system can rebuild the "T" cell and leukocyte counts to destroy the dysfunctional invading cells. All the physical programs are controlled by the mind's computer, or Subconscious Mind. The body is a hologram, so we must work with all levels—physical, mental, emotional, spiritual—at the same time. If we work on the physical body without understanding the root cause in the mind, the treatment will only be symptomatic and temporary. And if the emotional/ spiritual levels are not addressed, the problem will eventually recur in the same or another location in the body.

N/CR will access the root cause because it requires practitioners to get in contact with the feeling self. By doing so, we can listen to information in the Subconscious Mind which has been deposited in muscles/acupuncture points by the client's mind. Practitioners use acupuncture points for a switch to turn on the video/audio and allow the mind to bring the picture and experience up. This is where the similarity with other therapy processes stops. Since practitioners are able to listen to body/mind and go directly to the base cause, we get a clear understanding of what is causing the dysfunction. We describe the situation that caused the dysfunction, and then use an affirmation that the client repeats, thus permanently releasing the blockage. (My experience with Science of Mind helped me to understand and develop the affirmation part of N/CR. This is the key and the most important part to releasing and filing the record, program and pattern. N/CR is continually evolving, and we constantly upgrade the process as we verify the results.)

The focus of most therapy today, regardless of the modality, is to release or suppress the symptoms, but, unfortunately, that will not heal the body. Most practitioners expect the end result of their treatment to be some form of remission, cure or healing but, again as stated above, if you do not access the root cause, the treatment will be temporary and symptomatic. The body will always tell the truth no matter what we believe or even if we choose not to believe it. We always find that fear, anger and rejection are the base causes; yet we are always trying to blame some outside incident, person, or virus. The mind can create any disease it chooses; the only process that heals is *love*. With N/CR, we are allowing clients a safe space to learn how to love themselves and release the blockages in the body. In doing this, you will free yourself to receive the basic needs of all people—love, acceptance, approval, and alrightness that produce self-esteem and self-worth.

Your body is your mind. As a result, all negative experiences are locked into your body and will cause emotional reactions until they are recognized and released. Many people recognize the need to release emotional/physical memory but few achieve results. *All disease, illness, and dysfunctional emotional behavior patterns are directly caused by the lack of ability to accept oneself as alright and give and receive love! We can heal anything with love.* To reverse the process, we must understand unconditional love and accept its relationship to healing.

After I discovered the process 25 years ago, describing what NeuroCellular Repatterning™ was proved difficult. I had spent 20 years wandering through working allopathic doctors and then studying all the alternatives to allopathic medicine, looking for a cure for my own physical problems. I was not able to find one person who could understand my problem or alleviate my pain. I thought nutrition might be the key, but found it was only part of the solution. When I discovered the power of the mind, I realized it was not what you put in your mouth but what your mind accepts as truth that matters. This caused me to look for a healing modality that could get to the base cause of dysfunctions without having to spend hours trying to dig out the cause from a person who was unable to understand it in the first place. Most people don't know what their mind has stored, let alone understand it. I did not at that time connect my physical pain to emotional dysfunctional programs within my mind. I thought all physical problems had only physical origins … at least that's what the doctors told me. Yet they were not able to understand why my spine was deteriorating. I was told that if it did not stop, I would end up in a wheel chair, but they found no specific cause.

I decided that psychology might have the answer. In my training, conventional psychology seemed to be satisfied to blame it on someone or an unknown factor. I could not accept that we had to be victims of another person's reaction. I also did not know that my body was continually running a dialogue with me. If I had listened, it would have revealed the causes to me. In my training with Paul Solomon, we approached psychology from a holistic spiritual aspect. This was a very different slant from my original training. This did answer some of my questions, helping me understand the dialogue, but it did not heal my body.

In a workshop with Ronald Beesley, I was able to understand how the body stores the memory and the basics of removing it. With this knowledge, I had the tools to integrate spiritual psychology with body/mind therapy. This became the missing link that I incorporated into N/CR as the basis for my counseling. Even though I finally found the missing link, it took me another 20 years to complete the process we have now.

Physical dysfunctions reveal themselves, but not their causes. Emotional and mental pain are intangible, which makes locating and working with it difficult. I was unaware that my belief system had suppressed emotional programs that were causing my physical problem. Most people had no understanding or had any awareness of this syndrome until John Bradshaw made his entry on TV with the "dysfunctional family" programs. In my training, Fritz Perles and Virginia Satir approached this with different semantics, but it was the same syndrome. AA started the program but it did not become accepted until Codependency and Adult Children of Alcoholics and many others came along.

When I started in psychology and hypnosis, we were told that the Subconscious Mind was where all the power was and that ego was located in the Subconscious Mind. Ego was the enemy that we had to control. In fact most people accepted the notion that ego and Subconscious Mind had 88% control of our mind and Conscious Mind had only 12% control. I have discovered that it's the total opposite. Conscious Mind and Inner Conscious Mind have 100% control. Subconscious Mind is just a database for our memory. Ego is just a file manager and is located in Middle Self. It has no control over anything nor does it have an agenda to control us or anyone else. We also discovered there are four operating systems that are not in alignment with each other, and each one of these can and will sabotage us all the time. We found that it was very simple to reprogram all these mind's operating systems and change any dysfunction behavior.

As we went along, we discovered there many programs that we could clear with general affirmations because everybody had these conditions active in their mind. The affirmations in this book originated from my work with clients. I set up a series of standard affirmations to use with every person so that we can speed up the process. This was possible once we found that everybody had basically the same types of program present. With this, we can now reprogram any dysfunctional behavior, illness, disease or any program that is blocking abundance, success, peace, happiness, harmony and joy.

We have discovered that most people are operating from a split personality that is totally separate from true self. This personality self controls our life, yet we don't even know who it is. It is very simple to heal the separation from self and recover our lost self, yet we do not know we are separated; 95% of my clients are operating from split personalities, which is what people often term "a lost soul" or "splintered spirit." Neither term is accurate. Our souls and spirit are watching us, ready to guide us when we decide to listen. When we recover our lost self, true self is able to emerge. We can get back on track to success, peace, happiness, harmony, joy, unconditional love, and abundance in our life. Until we do, we will sabotage ourselves. You can use left brain analytical concepts to become successful if you use your will and push hard enough, using the proper mechanical systems and processes to become successful, but there is a catch. Are you willing to confront the issues in your life and take responsibility? Few people are, but those who do control the world.

This is the basic process of Energy Psychology for clearing the path to begin healing. Energy Psychology is the emotional release pattern to clear operational programs, whereas Energy Medicine is the second step to release the energy from the cellular memory programs in the acupuncture points along the meridian systems. Since the body is the mind, both Energy Psychology and Energy Medicine are intertwined. One does not work without the other.

We are removing all the negative, self-defeating software that limits or blocks a person's path to empowerment, self-worth, self-confidence, reclaiming personal power and self-esteem. When we remove or rewrite all the operating systems and backup files that our mind depends on for safety and security, Inner Conscious Mind can cause a relapse if it does not feel comfortable with our new path. When we first developed this process 20 years ago, we accepted the concept that ego and Subconscious Mind had 85% of the control. We have since discovered that this is simply not true. Conscious Mind and Middle Selves retain all the control. The question is what percentage of the whole are *we* in control of? Usually not very much. As you release and rewrite the all the operating systems in Middle Self, you will recognize the awesome power and control they have over your behavior.

Most people became lost in childhood, splintered and separated from who they really are due to fear and traumatic experiences. They escape into Magical Child to avoid the feelings of fear, pain, rejection and abandonment. When we separate from our true selves (Spirit and Soul), Conscious Mind splits into three separate operating systems. Conscious Rational Decision-Making Mind (who we should be operating from) shuts down, which activates Inner Conscious Mind and personality self. When we escape, somebody has to run the show, so our mind sets up split and multiple personality selves who run our life on autopilot through artificial intelligence, without our control. Since we are separated from true self, we are not aware that we don't have control over our mind and body.

As a result, the personality selves run our lives, since we have separated from true self and are not present in our life. Some people shut down completely and live in an emotionless survival with no feelings. They shut themselves off from life so they do not feel pain.

Most people will disagree we are lost and struggling in survival, yet it is documented in our research. The challenge is to get back to our true clear self, and erase the separation within ourselves. Until April, 2003, it was a hit-and-miss situation because, if we could not get the Conscious Mind to cooperate, we were unable to clear the separation. (Since my book *Your Body Is Talking; Are You Listening?* was revised and published in January, 2003, this information is not in it.)

Discovering that split personalities were taking up residence in the Conscious Mind solved the puzzle, and gave us the keys to how the mind operates. Split and multiple personalities are the keys to the challenge of correcting human behavior. We have avoided this subject in the past, as we felt that was the area for mental health professionals. Mental dysfunction was an area very few people understand. We have the key to correcting every level of a person's life that is malfunctioning. The trick is to convince clients to take responsibility and clear the separation from self. The magic of taking control of one's life is something that we cannot force upon a person. The problem is that fear will overpower and prevent a person from taking control and reclaiming his personal power. Each person is responsible to take this step him or herself. We can show you where the blocks are that cause the breakdown and separation, but we cannot remove them unless you make the decision and follow through with the intent to take responsibility and release the separation from self.

There are many payoffs in clinging to illness, disease and all the myriad malfunctions that cause chronic fatigue, depression, mental dysfunction and other debilitation that our mind provides. Many people struggle and suffer, assuming that this is the way it is going to be, never realizing they are creating their life path. We all are entitled to peace, happiness, harmony, joy, unconditional love and acceptance. We are also entitled to an abundance of success and wealth in everything we do. Very few people are able to recognize this and claim their abundance and prosperity.

As with peeling an onion, we find layers of consciousness covering layers below and we must clear each plateau before we get to the next one. The same goes for past lives. Sometimes we cannot get to a past life until all the layers involving prior past lives are cleared. Past life karma will create fear of approaching a particular situation, so we avoid it but don't understand why. Split personalities control and block us so we cannot even access the files. If we could get through all the barriers and doors that block us from achieving total abundance in our life, we could have it all effortlessly.

In some sessions, a client may just slog along, session after session, with very slow change. Yet, another client, with the same indications, may fly and accomplish twice or three times as much. It all depends on the client's willingness to change and ability to take the blinders off. There may be people you cannot help at all because, quite often, their body feels like a turtle shell. They will tell you they have no sensitivity at all. You *may* be able to break down the fear by using intuitive sensing and going through the session as if it were normal even though it feels that you are getting nowhere, and then the next session is normal.

Many people describe N/CR as magic because it releases pain on the spot without any manipulation or force. Every step in N/CR practice is explainable and requires no psychic healing or laying on of hands, because we can describe exactly what responses the minds are recording and what effect the work is having on the body.

Changing the programming changes the cellular structure, all the way down to the DNA level. Thoughts and feelings affect the body, locking in an energy component that changes the structure and weakens the muscles and the organs of the body. A simple affirmation will signal the mind to let go of the locked in energy and begin healing our body at a cellular level, changing the DNA structure. The resulting effect is described as Energy Medicine.

When we put our finger on the acupuncture point and couple it with an affirmation, cellular memory is released. Quite often the point will be painful, but only while the pressure is applied. The acupuncture point is like a switch that turns on the VCR in the Subconscious Mind and selects the tape applicable to the point we are working on. As the program, pattern and image come up, we can sense what it is and receive feedback similar to thought processing. If the incident has considerable impact, the picture can also be projected, like watching a movie or TV. At this point, we describe it to the client and discuss it. Then using the appropriate affirmation will release the program. Sometimes we get an incomplete release, so the pain persists. In this case, we continue with similar affirmations.

Most people feel that they must have all the affirmations written out so they can use them properly. I used to feel that way, too, but my experience has shown that people who have the confidence in themselves will be able to let their mind create the affirmation that is appropriate for their situation and application.

In the same way, clients will often question how they can access their clairvoyant abilities. (Psychic ability is not the same as clairvoyant ability. Psychics process information through their third chakra, which can color or place their own feelings in the reading. Clairvoyance uses the sixth and seventh, or crown chakra, which will yield more accurate information.)

Our process to learn this is very simple to learn, yet many people make it complicated and feel they are unable to practice. As a result, they water the technique down so it will not be so threatening to them. In N/CR, the practitioner cannot escape his/her own issues in the therapy process. In most schools of thought or therapy processes, you can easily escape your own issues by directing the process away from your own issues. Until you are willing to claim your personal power and confront all the issues in your life, they will continue to pop up in client sessions. In N/CR, you cannot avoid any of your issues because so many clients will mirror back your limitations. When we become aware of the issue, we can become detached so that we can use will to consciously keep control of the situation. I have noticed that when I work an issue completely through, I become nonattached to any triggers that used to set me off in the past. When the issue is worked out, I no longer get tested because the people who created the challenges are no longer in my life or they are no longer responding the same way.

Many of us think our life is working well until we run into the wall of resentment, anger or fear that we have been stuffing or suppressing. We cannot blame anybody as we knew what we were getting into when we took on a body. Since I have been in recovery, I recovered my lost self and the flight plan. I do not need to search for meaning in life anymore. We can look at the process of healing in a different light now. You do not have to be sick to know that you are not in wellness.

N/CR is not for everybody, because it puts your issues right in your face. When we release all the mind's back-up programs, there is no place to hide. You must look at them straight on. If you are not ready to face them, you will find a reason to discount the therapist or the process, or justify the issue even though there is no justification of any issue. You either want to clear it or live with it. When you clear an issue, it no longer causes any response or reaction.

The intent of N/CR is to desensitize a person, rewrite the dysfunctional software in the mind, install new programs and release the cellular memory that causes the dysfunctional behavior. When we accept "what is," life becomes much more comfortable. There is no need to judge, control, justify, criticize, or try to make another person meet our expectations of the situation. If their behavior is not to our liking, we tell them so with "I" statements. ("You" statements trigger an immediate reaction to protect or justify the self.)

If a client unloads a large amount of energy, it can cause the practitioner's circuit breakers to blow momentarily. This can cause a short "brown-out" until you recover your balance. There is also an issue with mental blockers and black-out programs that will work against us when we are working with clients. I discovered these programs the hard way when I kept passing out while driving. Many single-car crashes may be caused by people blacking out. It may feel like going to sleep, but in my experience, we do not have control over it. When I cleared the program, I did not have any more effects. I also discovered that black-outs would happen when I did not want to do a task before me. When I located the fear blocking me, the black-out programs were easy to delete and destroy.

Many people report that they have not run into this black-out problem. I think it depends how much you get into the process. We have now found that in addition to entities, we may have a person with a powerful mind that wants to control his life and has been given permission to do so. At first we did not understand how the mind controlled such a vast number of programs, but we recently discovered how the Middle Self works with the control sub-personalities. The power of the mind is so awesome that it can knock people out without their knowledge. This happened to me when I working with a client whose Instinctual Mind controlled her life 100%. I was sitting in a chair across the room from her and she knocked me out. When I discovered she had given up the will to live, I realized why her mind attacked me so intensely. Three weeks later, she died from undisclosed causes. Now that we understand how the process works, we no longer experience the therapist being knocked out.

In the past, many people viewed the N/CR process as almost mechanical. You release this program by holding the proper acupuncture point and repeat the affirmation applicable to the situation, and it clears the pain. Very little discussion went on during a session. Since the therapist was running the session, some clients felt they had little input. This was true in a way. I now recognize that clients want some time to respond to what we are releasing. If it is something they're not aware of, they may want to talk about it. I now direct the session but I no longer control it. There is a need for training in Energy Psychology so that practitioners can guide a client in the right direction in the transformational process and provide direction within the process. (That is now part of the training in workshops.)

In spring 1993, we found a block that I did not understand, because I did not realize the power of the Instinctual Mind. We have discovered that the Instinctual Mind becomes operative only when a person gives up in life or has had a traumatic experience in which the Instinctual Mind installs *"I want to die"* programs that will stay in the file until they are removed. Medical and brain researchers describe this as the Limbic Mind. According to them, it is an animal/reptilian-like mind. Once I got a handle on it, I found it easy to deal with. The Instinctual Mind works from programming only. It is the "survival self," and views every action in a survival mode, but just change the programming and uninstall its operating system and instructions, and it will comply. It cannot make rational decisions or understand any commands other than its programming. It works through the Conscious Mind rather than the Subconscious Mind. It can act with the Subconscious Mind in a survival mode. Since the events of September 11, 2001, this has all changed. Now, 99 out of 100 people have been pushed into survival mode by the disaster. People could not deal with the trauma, which pushed them beyond their ability to handle stress.

I also discovered the power of the Conscious Mind and willpower. With enough willpower, the Conscious Mind can overcome the Subconscious Mind's programs. It will take enormous energy and the person will feel burned out, but it can be done. This is why people with life-threatening diseases live against all odds. We use Neuro-Kinesiology as a directional device that a person can use to track down the situation in the beginning. We have found it to be a useful tool in locating and reprogramming concepts and beliefs that have no programs tied to them. When I studied with Dr. John Diamond in the 1970s, I did some work with Behavioral Kinesiology, which I found interesting but did not include in N/CR until fifteen years later. We have now refined it into what we call Neuro-Kinesiology. In 1991, I incorporated the testing for electrical polarity reversals as part of the testing because I found that a polarity reversal causes all answers received using kinesiology to be reversed. *Yes* will appear as *No* and *No* as *Yes*. When we clear this, the testing reverts back to normal. In the 1970s, I learned a simple Chinese process and included it in the process in 1991.

With the effects of walking out of the body becoming more common now, I have had to find a remedy for this. In 1992, I put together a new affirmation to pull people back into their body. A client who couldn't stay in her body when I was working with her helped me create the affirmation to pull a person back into the body. When you confront something during sessions that clients do not want to deal with, they will walk out, something we term "graying out." Clients sense this when you make them aware of their reaction. Eventually this will be easy for clients to recognize, and saying the affirmation will pull them right back into the body.

The purpose of Energy Psychology is to locate the blocks and the limitations that cause breakdowns in the body and mind, so we can release the energy driving the illness, disease and the dysfunctional habit patterns. Energy Medicine is the release of the cellular memory that is locked into the acupuncture points along the meridians in the muscles and fascia tissue of the body. It can get locked into organs in the body, too, which causes breakdowns in the organs and the endocrine system.

Most people live in survival, fear, resentment and anger. Our intention is to get 100% control back so we can function as the spiritual being we are. We were intended to operate in wholeness, but if we are separated, splintered and blocked out from our true self, we are lost.

When we reclaim our power, we set an intention and goal to be consistent with our commitment to follow through.

You also may be tested by your inner teacher to see if you have taken control over your life. Temptations will be presented to you in order to test your ability to see if you will fall back into the old pattern. If you pass the test and retain your personal power, you will not be tested again. On the other hand, if you fail the test, it will throw you back into survival. We can create the same patterns over again and fall back into survival, which activates Instinctual Mind files. If this happens, it will shut down file and program manager operating systems. It will also shut off the love program. This may reactivate personality selves, inner Conscious Mind and shadow selves. If this happens, read the Instinctual Mind affirmation and check that file and program manager systems have been reactivated. Check the other files to make sure nothing has been reinstalled. This must be done at the beginning of each session. The intent is to clear all the programs and sub-personalities and reclaim our personal power.

The result of using these two disciplines precipitates to Psychoneuro-immunology, which is the study of what happens when negative energy gets locked in the cellular structure of the body. The brain/mind runs bi-directional pathways in the body that communicate with the cellular structures using neuropeptides, serotonins and cytokinins. These chemicals and many other brain/mind controlled chemicals can provide health and well being or can break our body down in minutes.

When you are asking questions from the Subconscious Mind you could miss the accurate answers if information is suppressed in the time-lines, back-up files, or in denial or denial-of-denial. (Time-lines are the year that a traumatic experience happened.) When the incident is negative and traumatic, the mind does not want to deal with this incident, so it drops it into denial so you do not have to deal with it again. If a lesson has been brought up to deal with and you refuse to acknowledge the lesson, it will be put in denial-of-denial, so it's locked up and will not come up again. It may also have been linked to an autopilot file that a controller sub-personality was using at the time, so when it was suppressed into the denial file, the autopilot went with it. These must be removed or they will control a person's life. We have recently discovered that programs can be deposited in future time-lines, which puts them out of reach in current time. You must ask if a program is contained in future time-lines.

When all these tests are made, you can be reasonably sure that you can make direct contact with Higher Self and the Subconscious Mind. If you want to go on-line with the Akashic Internet, you simply connect the phone lines by asking your higher self and the Highest Source of your being to connect you. You then can ask questions that are not body-based.

If you choose to use a pendulum, you may run into interference from astral entities, or from entities within yourself or the client. (They can control pendulums without you even knowing it.) It will appear that the answers are correct, but they are controlled by other forces. We have experienced this many times over the past 20 years. Brass pendulums seem to work best because they are heavier and will be influenced less. Many excellent books are in print on pendulums and dowsing, and we recommend *Improve Your Life Through Dowsing* by David Allen Schultz (we publish and distribute this book).

The first step with a pendulum is to determine how the pendulum is going to swing. Ask your mind to give you the directions for *yes* and *no*. Remember the pendulum is just an extension of your mind, and you are projecting the answer out to the pendulum instead of getting it clairvoyantly or through your intuition. Ask to indicate a *no* and a *yes*. The swing will be your guide. Most people will get to-and-fro swings, back-and-forth swings, or circles. You must practice to see what your *yes* and *no* motion will be. As you work with the pendulum, you will find there are more answers in addition to *yes* and *no*, such as doubtful, not available, etc.

With neuro-kinesiology, you are getting the information from the person through a muscle reaction instead of using your own intuition. Quite often when working with a client, you will get more accurate answers with muscle-testing because you will not be filtering it through your mind, which could color the answers if you have strong beliefs, interpretations or feelings about the subject in question.

Control sub-personalities may interpret letting go as giving up their power. You may have to assure Middle Self that it is not losing anything, but is instead gaining new power because you are reclaiming your personal power. It may glory in the fact that it can manipulate you. Inner Conscious mind really likes the fact it could control your life and it feels threatened because it has to give up control. If that happens, then all sub-personalities must be deleted from the file before you can claim control. This is a process that takes training and experience, so you will must practice this process. The most important factor is being clear of outside or inside influences. You can control the answers very easy if you do not want to do a particular task or if you are unaware that there is resistance in your Conscious Mind.

We have found two new aspects of the mind we were not aware of in the past. Conscious Mind has two divisions (see Appendix A for details):

- Conscious Rational Mind, and
- Inner Conscious Mind.

Middle Self has an Inner operating system, too. Both of them seem to be the autopilot function and many times will resist change if they feel you will not follow through with your commitment and discipline yourself to make the change. They can reinstall programs very easily without your knowledge.

This does not mean that sub-personalities will never be reinstalled since your Conscious Mind can recreate a new set anytime you do not take responsibility to follow through with the decisions you have chosen to act upon. Your mind does not like unfinished answers or sentences, or uncompleted actions or commitments. Do not say you are going to do something unless you intend to follow through. If you do not follow through, your mind will assume you did not want to act on the decision you made. If you do not take action, your mind has to close that program. This closure will create a sub-personality and a program about not wanting to take action. If it happens often enough, avoider, confuser, procrastinator, disorientor and disorganizer sub-personalities get installed, along with a "not wanting to take responsibility" sub-personality. It can go on and on if you get into indecision and back away from taking action on the path you were choosing to take responsibility for. Any time you make a commitment that you do not follow through with, it creates a program that is interpreted as, "I am not willing to take control of my life." If this happens over a number of years, your Instinctual Self will interpret this as, "I want to die."

Your mind will not leave any loose ends unattended, and has to have closure on every thought, statement or action you take. Even if you start a sentence without finishing it, will complete the sentence for you. So every thought and action you create must be completed or your mind will finish it and file it. It is on 24/7 and is a very good housekeeper, but it may not complete the file the way you would have done.

A program creates a sub-personality and will drive that sub-personality to get the desired result. If self-rejection is carried to the final stage, it will create a life-threatening illness. There may be disease specific sub-personalities that were created with the disease or dysfunctional program or belief. A disease, illness or dysfunction cannot exist in the body without a program to drive it. There must be some activating force to break down the immune system or cause stress on the adrenals or the endocrine system. Any form of negative thought or action will start an immediate breakdown in the immune and the endocrine systems. Receptor sites on the leukocytes are notified in microseconds by the neuropeptides. This begins a physical deterioration of the immune and endocrine systems, which in turn causes the beginning of illness and disease as the immune system function is compromised and fewer T-cells and leukocytes are produced.

When releasing programs, make sure that you check for the sub-personalities that could be enabling them. Each time you clear a time-line or operating file, it may activate another series that has been set to be brought up in position from a back-up file or a denial file.

When clearing karmic files, check for gate-keepers, guards and saboteurs that can be connected with the files. They will try to block release of the files. They can be cleared in the same way as attached spirit beings.

If a person degenerates or sets up *I want to die* programs, the control of the mind/body shifts to the Instinctual Mind. Programs can set up in this mind when this takes place. Any conflict in the mind about *fear of dying* and *I want to die* will set up sub-personalities in the Survival Self (Middle Self). This conflict is the main cause of Alzheimer's disease; these two programs cause an Alzheimer's file to be created, which must be cleared before the person begins the backward slide or it becomes very difficult to stop.

When clearing, you must clear all denial and denial-of-denial programs and sub-personalities. You can bring them up by asking with kinesiology if this program is a belief and then a reality. If it comes up positive on both, then ask Holographic Mind to go through all the veils, shields and illusions into the back-up files, time-line files, the denial and denial-of-denial files, bringing them up all the hidden files to the surface and reveal the true answers. If it continues to come up positive, you have a program that is locked into the physical body. If the reality question comes up weak, then you have a denial. Check for them and clear them from all files. In cases where there has been trauma, it will create time-lines that can be in denial, also. They can also be in autopilot, in denial or denial-of-denial.

We must also check for reactivator, recreator, regenerator, reduplicator and reinstaller programs or viruses that will create the same program again and again. These will be attached to individual programs so you must check each program for this each time you clear the program and sub-personality. We have also found another program that can recreate sub-personalities and programs. Similar to a computer virus, this program only functions when activated by a word, an activity, a feeling or an emotion. It will activate a program that will run its course and then close down. If you do not catch it during its operational cycle, it disappears. The results or effects of its activity will remain, but we cannot find out how this situation was created until we discovered how to ask the proper questions to reveal it. We found another virus that acts in the same as a regenerator, which we described as an activator virus. It can create or activate existing programs that may be dormant, such as an allergy. (This is the reason we go through such an extensive process of releasing, deleting and destroying dysfunctional software programs.)

Each time you are in session with a client, clear the sub-personalities. This will indicate how the client is doing in taking responsibility in their life. Each time we get into a situation where we do not handle it properly, Middle Self and Conscious Mind will install controller and many other sub-personalities that apply to the situation in which we lost control.

The number of sub-personalities and programs that reoccur over time reveals our progress in handling our life path. Once we clear all the sub-personalities, some will be recreated depending upon our ability to handle the situations that come up in our life. When we are able to handle all situations without losing our center, needing to be right, being in power and control, giving our power away or following through with all our intentions and commitments, our mind will not install sub-personalities. Anger or resentment will open emotional doors, so programs and sub-personalities will be installed. The ideal is to get to a point where no sub-personalities are installed. When this occurs, you will have 100% control over your life.

Each time we conduct a session, the controller sub-personalities must be checked. If they keep reoccurring, we need to find out why a person is not taking full responsibility for their life. You may find that they just do not want to take control or discipline themselves. We have found very few first-time clients who are actually in control of their life. Many who claim to be, based on all the seminars, workshops, training and therapy they have participated in or taken, but in most cases, little has changed. However, we must be careful not to judge or criticize what a person has done in the past. They did the best they could with the tools and awareness they had at the time.

Taking responsibility is a very big issue in everyone's life. We said we had some answers in the past, but we could not actually describe how you take responsibility in your life. We can now, as we have found all the programs, beliefs and sub-personalities that block a person. One of the major blocks is plain laziness. When we have cleared all the blocks, it comes down to the individual's desire, which is controlled by Conscious Mind. If clients do not *want* to apply personal control and become self-actualized, there is nothing we can do as practitioners to change that situation. You can ask all the questions you want and receive many answers, but are they the correct answers? Highly unlikely if you are not clear of the controllers in your mind.

Since the last printing of this manual we have discovered a massive amount of information about how the mind controls our life. We thought we had the answer when we found Magical Child Syndrome but it was only the tip of the iceberg. The discovery of Inner Conscious Mind and the personality selves opened the door to how the mind controls us. Finding the violent birth experience opened another door to why we lose our self-esteem and self-worth.

In the past we assumed when a person fell back and could not maintain their control and retain their personal power, it was their fault for not disciplining themselves to stay on top of their mind control. We have found that is not the case. There is a battle going on in our mind to stop us from taking control. Personality selves will recreate sub-personalities and programs with the help of Middle Self to maintain control.

Now that we can remove all the back-up programs and the virus recreation and reinstaller programs that the mind used to maintain control, it will indicate when a person is not taking responsibility. People will fall back into survival when incidents come up that they cannot handle or threaten them. It can be as simple as a thought that you are unsure of how to handle a situation. Or if someone is negative towards you and you accept what they say as an attack or rejection, you will go into survival. By checking the incident and when it happened, we get an accurate view of what is blocking a client from taking control in their life. We can locate the incident and track it down, to the day and hour.

The mind assumes everything is happening now, and it cannot recognize the past unless you describe the incident in the past. Therefore, when talking about past experiences, you must speak in third person and use past tense, or your mind will assume the incident is happening now and will attempt to protect you.

Resistance can be very hard to overcome, as can getting out of the rut of autopilot. Also procrastination will throw you into survival. To break a habit or a pattern, sometimes we must use the 21-day writing affirmation to burn in the concept until the mind gives in and allows us to take control of your life.

We do not judge where a person is at on the individual path. Their body/mind will reveal that to us. The path a person decides to take is totally up to them. All we can provide is guidance and the software to rewrite our life scripts. N/CR cannot force a person to take control over their life.

We are releasing the imbedded cellular memory from past experiences. Each cell has a memory of the perfect image of how it can regenerate itself. If there is no dysfunctional negative overlay of emotional energy blocking, all cellular structures will regenerate perfectly from the blueprint each time the cells are rebuilt. I have seen many miracles with clients, but was unsure of how it actually took place.

There is hope. Recovery is possible in every case. The only catch is the desire to take control and discipline yourself to do what it takes. I am a walking example of a miracle. In my book *Your Body Tells the Truth*, I document many case histories of people who literally shifted their belief and were healed in minutes. Some it took days to years, depending on their willingness to let go of attachment to the cause and the core issues that have manifested the dysfunction. All of them are the same; *The root cause in any dysfunction of the body or the mind is anger, fear or rejection, which results in lack of love.* When the connection to Source is restored, love can begin to heal the body/mind.

Control is the most widespread addiction we have today. It is insidious in the way we react to it, both as therapists and clients. If you are not in recovery, it is not an issue. Many people in recovery do not recognize it as an issue either. If we have an expectation of how a program, meeting, or how a person should respond, we seek to control. As therapists, we are only able to guide and help clients understand the causes and core issues that are causing the dysfunction in their lives. The biggest challenge comes if they cannot receive love or love themselves. If love does not exist in a person's reality, how does he or she recover self-esteem and self-worth, let alone heal themselves? When we separate from our Source, we shut off the presence of God within.

Chapter 3

The Transition to
Psychoneuroimmunology (PNI)

About ten years ago, I heard about PNI but it did not register because it was a medical concept. When I researched PNI, Energy Psychology and Energy Medicine, I discovered they were right in line with Neuro/Cellular Repatterning.

In 1974 Robert Ader, a psychiatrist and instructor at the University of Rochester Medical School, became interested in how the brain interacts with the body and the immune system. In 1987, the Dept. of Behavioral Medicine was established at Yale University to research PNI.

Ader now has his own department to research and teach behavioral medicine and PNI at Rochester University Medical Center. In their research over the years, they found something I have contended since I began working in this field. The body/mind is an integrated unit. What affects one part will have an effect on all aspects of the body, but 25 years later, researchers still have yet to introduce PNI into medical or psychological practice. Some practitioners claim to be using it, yet I have found from what I have read of their work it is hit and miss ... which brings in the placebo effect. (The placebo effect depends on the client's *belief* in the product, process or practitioner. If they accept the effectiveness of the practitioner's work and/or the product, it will work.)

We are in the forefront of a paradigm shift in alternative medicine. In an attempt to understand immuno-regulatory function, PNI researchers have set up laboratory studies to test negative impact on the mind and body. Converging data from different disciplines have provided compelling evidence that negative emotions and sensory feedback in the form of verbal attack does, in fact, cause immediate changes that break down the body. As with any other systems working to create homeostasis, the body, the immune and endocrine systems are integrated with other psycho-physiological processes, and researchers found that the brain interacts with the body. Bingo! We have a new avenue to research. But, they have not yet found out how to control the interactions in this stimulus/response immuno-regulatory system. We have a system and a process that meet this need with N/CR, Energy Psychology and Energy Medicine.

The battle lines seem to be building as the conventional orthodox researchers have bristled at the notion that there's a connection between the brain and the immune system, despite the replicated studies that have found such a link. Critics claim they have yet to find a biological mechanism linking the two systems. Ader states that does not bother him, as there are many medical and psychological phenomena where we cannot yet define the precise mechanisms. In a keynote presentation before the American Immunological Association, he said that if we could put the concepts of PNI to work, it would have a depressive effect on the practices of the audience. But he assured them that this would not happen, as people do not want to take responsibility for their health and we have not found a way to build a person's self-image to put PNI to work in an effective manner yet.

Many researchers are finding that psychology, medicine, religion and spirituality overlap. In some cases, they find that people with a strong faith and belief in religion and/or spirituality seem to recover faster from illness. People who tend to be enthusiastic, happy and optimistic seem to recover faster also. They find that the Pavlovian studies of many years ago tend to bear out the fact that people who recognize a negative factor will avoid it, and that tends to support recovery and preventive health.

This book documents and describes how we approach every form of illness, disease and behavioral dysfunction at the Energy of Psychology level. Book Two in the series documents how we handle all the dysfunctions at the body level with Energy Medicine and N/CR. We have built the wellness model and we can put it to work with 100% effectiveness. Our inclusive package provides direction and information on all four tracks 1. Physical Health, 2. Mental/Emotional Health, 3. Financial Health and 4. Spiritual Health. It also documents preventive practices to avoid the above, besides being a compendium of ways to create and maintain perfect health. It covers all methods to build psychological, mental, physical and spiritual balance in one's life. We will see if this breaks into the field of medical and psychological practices.

Neuro/Cellular Repatterning proves without a doubt that the mind does control the body functions and we can heal anything if the person is willing to reprogram the mind's functions. Not only that; we can also create a balance whereby a person can avoid stress and physical/mental breakdowns.

Basically PNI is the study of the interrelationship and the link between the brain (mind) and the immune/endocrine systems. The sympathetic nervous system and the autonomic nervous systems are the major carriers along with the brain chemicals neuropeptides and the cytokinins. These are bidirectional in their action. If you feel good and have a positive mental image of yourself, they support your endocrine and immune systems. If you are pessimistic and have negative feelings about yourself, they work against you and suppress your immune and endocrine systems. Depression can be the result of long term negativity.

Scientific researchers are trying to create a wellness model that will support a positive mental image, thereby creating health and wellness. The only problem is that they are missing the main point. The mind runs on programs and you cannot force a positive pattern on a person who has negative programs breaking them down. Visualization, guided imagery, meditation and biofeedback can help but they will not change the programs. A few people can rewrite programs by practicing a belief over and over until their mind writes over the dysfunctional program, but that does not mean the base cause has been cleared, and the program could be recreated at a later date. This takes time and few people will discipline themselves to spend time to follow through.

In Carl Simonton's work, he has had what many people would call great success, but I differ in that it seems to me that his rate of healing of cancer was only partially successful over the last 25 years. Some medical doctors are beginning to experiment with PNI and a few who have discovered that all healing is placebo effect. I met a doctor at Book Expo America who had written a book on placebo effect. He claimed that now he is using sugar pills and saline water, he is 50% more effective than when he practiced allopathic medicine.

We feel we will be able to build a wellness model that will prove that we are setting up a program that will provide long term results as they have over the last twenty years.

The release of the documentry movie *What the Bleep Do We Know?* has opened a new door that will convey what I've been trying to bring forth for the last twenty years.

Chapter 4

Cracking The Mind's Codes

Since we are multifaceted, binary digital computer, every file directory is coded and locked in the Subconscious Mind's data base. We do not hear or see with visual impressions or words; all our sensory input is transmitted through chemical reactions or electrical impulses through neuro pathways in our body. The brain is a switching network that directs all the information to the various cellular points of contact. Our concern is our mind, not just the brain. The seat of our intuitive ability is in the solar plexus also known as the third chakra.

The information is transmitted in microseconds from thought to action. We have control over how the information is interpreted and used to get the end result we desire, yet very few people use their ability to maintain control of their body and mind. About 90 percent of the population is on autopilot, and as a result have very little control over their daily activities. Almost all of their reactions are automatically decided by their Inner Conscious Mind with help from the sub-personalities. Our database in our Subconscious Mind contains all the sub-directories with all the files and programs which are used to direct our daily life. They can be accessed in microseconds.

One of limitations we have to deal with is that the Conscious Mind can only record sensory input at 134 bits per second, which is very slow compared to the Subconscious Mind at 210 million bits per second. We can teach ourselves to bypass the Conscious Mind's limitations by learning how to scan. In a technique called Photo Reading, we can read a 100-page book in 20 to 30 minutes.

We must also understand that our Subconscious Mind never turns off; it is on 24/7, recording every bit of sensory input that makes contact with it, whether we want it to or not. We can maintain some control by setting up programs to block certain input, and in the later steps in this manual, you will install a quarantine, firewall and "spamblocker" that will help sort out or block information that is not in the best interests of our health and well being.

We can choose how we desire to respond to every thought and sensory input, yet very few people understand how this happens. In a sense, we are at the mercy of our mind's programs and most people do not even know it, so they justify or blame everything around them. Every minute of the day, either we can have total control of our life or give our personal power away.

Often we see the person who has unlimited energy and enthusiasm, and seems to flow effortlessly through life with no limitations. Everything seems to fall into place for them with no restrictions. How does that happen? I have direct experience with the situation myself. Twenty years ago, it seemed that I would never get to this point in my path where life was ease instead of a struggle and a battle. I knew from my research over the last 25 years you must build a solid foundation. I tried to find how to do this by studying as many alternative therapy processes I could, and became a "workshop junkie." I never found the answer until 1982 when I bought a computer.

When I started my journey, I did not know there are four sets of codes that must be mastered to get to the state of enlightenment I was seeking. To build the foundation for success, I decided I had find the way to total wellness. Everybody told me they had the answer. Looking for this elusive key to success, I wandered through all the various disciplines from Eastern to Western gurus and teachers, but never found it. When John Bradshaw came along in 1988 with his concept about how dysfunctional families affect our lives, it opened the door to understanding what I had been running into with clients.

My physical pain was driving my life but I did not find that key until 1984. In my attempt to find the answer, I cracked the first code to physical wellness and success in 1978 yet I did not know it at the time. I started maintaining my current age and becoming younger. I accomplished feats that people said I could not do. Even though I was feeling better, cracking the emotional/psychological code (#2) took six more years of research. In 1984, a client revealed to me how to crack the code. Working with her, I was able to heal my back pain. She was the catalyst to bring this awareness to me. I was sailing along with this new awareness that physical health is controlled by our mind until I met the next lesson. My business went bankrupt in 1987 because I was not watching the hen house, and the foxes (my partners) killed the business.

It took twelve more years until 1998 to crack the third code—mental control and success. When I recognized that there was nobody but me out there to show me how to succeed, I recognized the code. Many people had the formula, but I had to activate it in myself. I had released all the negating rejection and resentment programs from the past, so I assumed I should succeed. How do you step up to the home plate hit a home run? That was the elusive one for me.

In 1997 when I published my first book, I went stone deaf until I discovered the code. I realized there was a major file on "*people will not accept what I have to say, so why stick yourself out there, where you will fail?"* I would not give up because I knew I could make the grade. I presented a seminar while deaf, which really showed me I was accepted. Everybody was supporting me for not backing out and canceling my presentation. This opened the door, yet I was not finding the key to financial success. My mind was fighting with me because it felt it was protecting me from rejection. I finally broke this barrier in 2001 after going deaf two more times.

In 2003, we discovered another situation that exists in 99 percent of us—that we are not who we think we are. This was a major break through for me when one of my client-practitioners in Toronto, Canada told me we have to clear split- and multiple-personality selves. We could describe this as a code since the selves are set up in such a way that if you do not ask the proper question, they will not be revealed. See description in Step 4 of Chapter 10.

Most of us have been programmed as I was for failure. We carry "I am not all right," "I am not entitled to," "I am not accepted or approved of," plus fears of vulnerability, of being inadequate, of being rejected and/or abandoned, and myriad defective programs that cause us to react to get approval. We become saviors, rescuers and empathizers so we can draw approval from others. When I was able to break the third code everything opened up and I could see why I was limiting myself. The second and third codes are intertwined so must be cracked before real success can take place.

The fourth code is spiritual awareness. Most people start here and forget they have to build a foundation for success. I started at this point, too. In 1976, I decide to sell my restaurant to go on the journey to find myself. I was lost in this spiritual metaphysical jungle until I recognized that enlightenment involved activating all the codes in order. When I started showing people that the spiritual aspect was the last one, many people rejected my contention. Twenty years later they are still stuck in the mire of their disbelief … and envy of me. I showed them the way up the ladder when I was at their level but they did not want to take responsibility for their life.

Spiritual transformation only happens when you are capable of listening. This brings on the level of enlightenment where you realize that you get what you give. My books *Your Body Is Talking; Are You Listening?* and *Journey Into The Light* detail my work and research on the last code.

When you get to this step, you open the door to another series of lessons and codes that have be worked through. True success and abundance at all levels of your life can be accomplished when you release all the malfunctioning programs that block you from success and abundance.

Once you get the doors of success and abundance open, everything falls into place. It seems effortless as everybody and the universe seem to be at your service. Some people seem to ascend this ladder effortlessly, while others fight and struggle throughout their life. For a few people, the codes were opened when they were born so they inherited a functional family. They seem to live a charmed life, yet others from the same family never seem to succeed. Why? We carry forward our file cabinet from past lives, with all the unresolved lessons until we confront the issues. We must clear the lessons generated by our past lives or they will block our success.

Many people may not have to go through all the lessons as some of the codes may have been opened by their parents because they were shown what to be loved and acceptance was. They appear to go forward without much hindrance. Other people have the desire to create the intention and the commitment to discipline themselves to follow through, yet they never seem to make the grade. If they keep their commitment and have to fight themselves until they reach their goal, they will reprogram their mind to build a habit which will result in a belief that, in time, will overwrite the defective program. Many successful people have taken this route. It takes a considerable amount of drive and will power to accomplish the goal in this manner. I know I accomplished my goals by never giving up or letting myself fall back as a victim.

Over the years, I wondered and was puzzled by people who seemed to have it made financially. Their success and abundance were obvious, yet they had meltdowns, crashing and burning in the physical, emotional or relationship areas of their life. Most of these people would not talk with me or allow me to work with them because they assumed that their success in the financial arena was what defined "success." I discovered that they could not understand why they could be so successful financially, while their health was failing or their emotions were spiraling out of control. Going more deeply, I found that their focus was off base. We are multifaceted beings and must work with, and take care of, every level and every quadrant of our lives.

Why is it that only 5 percent of the population understands this process of success? We can go to endless seminars, workshops and boot camps on personal success and generate many streams of income, but will we follow through? Statistics show that less than 25 percent of the people who attend these seminars, etc., actually reach the goal of financial success. And less than 2 percent reach the level of total wellness at all levels of enlightenment. Why?

Most people get caught in procrastination, avoidance, confusion, vacillation, indecisiveness, disorientation, disassociation and inability to take action. Then they beat themselves up for not seeing that they could accomplish what they set out to do. Unfortunately, they are driven by the programs in their database in the Subconscious Mind.

When we have no resistance blocking us, we can set on the path to our goal. It starts with desire, intention, commitment, discipline, and the courage to follow through. When we get a few victories in our success file, we can see that it is very easy when there are no limiting programs.

How do we break down the limitations? Quite often, when I work with people who are committed to change, I discover they find that their mind blocks the change, and they will find reasons to cancel appointments, and come up with all manner of reasons to justify their actions. If we *do* get to have a session, their Conscious Rational Mind will try to throw them back into survival when they confront the change. Most of the time, I find this happens in the first 24 hours, if we have not uncovered and cleared special relationships in the Conscious Rational Mind.

These "special relationships" are the safety net we operate from that provides our acceptance and validation for stability in our life. When we remove these safety nets, there is no longer a sense of security, and it may cause us to go into a tailspin. This can bring up fear that is not understood, which in turn may cause a physical reaction that could result in fatigue, depression, or even a life-threatening illness. This may seem illogical, but we must understand that our mind is irrational and illogical when reacting to fear. All it perceives is loss of control, and will attempt to regain it, if we have not deprogrammed all the connections with special relationships or traumatic incidents that, in its perception, will reoccur if we continue reclaiming our personal power.

For self-righteous, controlling people who must be the authority or know-all, this threat to control becomes twice as hard to overcome. We have discovered that Conscious Rational Mind (CRM) is where what we call EGO related behaviour comes from. It always wants to be right. It will judge, justify, project blame and anything else it can use to justify being right. Thinking that it will lose perceived power, the mind will sabotage any attempts at change, and will bring about the very failure it feared would happen.

I have seen people who confront this pattern in their lives and become extremely sick or set up a life-threatening illness, crossing over in a few days. Our mind can be very controlling, to the point of causing us to die if we do not take control of our personal power. This may seem ironic, but we can cause ourselves to become sick or set up our own death when we confront our inability to reclaim our personal power. I have seen it happen many times with clients who are up against the wall but see the wall as impenetrable, and simply give up. It seems almost unreal that an illusionary wall could cause a person's death, but it can happen if they see themselves as a victim of their own circumstances.

I stress that we must balance our life in all four quadrants (see below) and build it on a solid foundation because, when we confront a situation that we must overcome, we can overcome the negative programming of feeling threatened. If we build the foundation to work from, it will not crumble when we confront an issue that seems intense.

Cracking this code was my ticket to freedom from the control exerted by my mind. I have found there is no silver bullet or a magical number of sessions that will allow us to become free, and who we really are. It is up to *us* to take control of *our* life in all four quadrants. No one can do it for us.

The Four Quadrants of Perfect Health

The four quadrants of a solid, balanced foundation for personal and financial success are:
1. Physical Health: nutrition, diet and exercise
2. Mental/emotional and psychological health
3. Financial health: prosperity and success
4. Spiritual health: understanding spiritual principles and connection with higher power/Source.

Chapter 5

Introduction to the Practice of Energy Psychology - Energy Medicine and Neuro/Cellular Repatterning

Before we begin an N/CR session, I explain the principles of N/CR to the client. Always explain, "I am not a healer and I do not work on them. This process requires that you and I work together."

Some clients object to any religious sounding words, so I have dropped the use of, "as the Christ master self that I am" to begin the affirmation. If you are working with somebody who objects, ask them to substitute whatever higher power they would like to use. If they do not want to use any preamble, start out the affirmation with "I recognize now …" It really makes no difference because we are working with a computer so the preamble is not as important as I used to believe it was.

When we track beliefs and concepts with Kinesiology we must clear the person before we can begin working because if there is an entity, a series of control sub-personalities or if Instinctual Mind has been activated, we may not get accurate answers. You may not be able to use muscle-testing if the arm becomes locked. The mind can be controlled and cause the arm to drop so you will think you have an accurate test.

Before you work with anyone, you must ground yourself because in N/CR, we are actually passing the negative energy through ourselves and neutralizing it in the ground. Follow the steps in Chapter 7 to get accurate results from our work. Use the steps in that chapter so that everything is cleared as we go through the process.

To enter the proper state for doing the work, you also need to center. This prepares you to receive guidance from the Presence of God within you. Without this guidance, you cannot properly do this work, especially the more advanced psychological aspects. It will move all of your communication above the astral plane to the 5th dimension or higher.

To begin, we must make sure we are clear and able to provide the energy and direction required to work in the session. This also means that we must be in recovery, working with and clearing our issues if we desire to be an effective practitioner. I will repeat this over and over: You cannot practice N/CR and treat other people without having first dealt with your own issues and blockages, releasing and clearing them. With almost any other alternative practice, you can avoid your own issues by sidestepping them, but not in N/CR, for they will come up during a session if the client has the same or similar issues as you. Working with a client with the same issues will catalyze your issues and bring them right up so you must deal with them.

If you have concerns about your credibility and how you present yourself to clients, you must clear as many of your basic issues as you can before you begin working with people. Further instructions regarding clearance will be found in Chapter Nine: Steps Practitioners Must Take.

Chapter 6

Affirmations: the Software

The purpose of this chapter is to give you a basic understanding of how effective affirmations are structured and the purpose of each part of the affirmation. As you will find, keeping these general structures in mind will speed your work and give you confidence in your own abilities. N/CR would not work effectively without affirmations. You can hold points for minutes to hours, which will achieve energy releases, but no more. You must locate the base cause, core issue and sometimes the catalyst, and then release the pattern and programs to release the dysfunctional program. Releases should take about 30 seconds to a few minutes.

Affirmations are the back bone of N/CR as they are the software that we use to rewrite old programs. The practitioner cannot rewrite the programs. No matter how hard you try to convince the client's mind to accept the affirmation, it will not always do this. The only person that can do this is the client. Nobody can reprogram you without your permission. You must accept the programming. If you are not in control of your mind and you have an authority figure program where you give your power away to people in authority, then another person can tell you something and your mind will accept it.

N/CR is a right-brained, feeling level process. We always ask the client to get into their feeling level and to not analyze the process. You may find some clients will resist repeating the affirmations. If this happens, ask them to help you in forming the affirmation.

The affirmations are the key to effectiveness of Energy Psychology, Energy Medicine and N/ CR. They are the way we talk to the Conscious Mind, Conscious Rational Mind, Program Manager (Middle Self), File Manager (Ego), Higher Self and the Subconscious Mind to get them to support releasing negative energy from the body. Often, however, the body you are working on may give you different affirmations than the ones listed here, and sometimes you will find that you are not even using the standard format. This is perfectly fine, because we are really interested in obtaining release of Subconscious Mind's negative programs, and improving the thought processes and taking back control from Conscious Rational Mind. Go with whatever is working!

~ ~ ~

Over the last 25 years, people tell me they've been told that all you need to do to set up an affirmation is describe what you want to accomplish and state the affirmation, over and over again. However, I have discovered in my research that our mind may be unable to accept the affirmation due to operating systems that will not allow it to be filed. Also, unfortunately, you cannot tell your mind what you want it to do if it is programmed with the opposite belief. An example is: *"I am entitled to money. Money is coming into my reality now. I see it coming to me now. I am accepting money in my life now. I have wealth in my life now."*

Our mind's response to this affirmation is: "So *where is the money?"* You keep repeating the affirmation over and over in hopes that it will work, yet money does not seem to manifest. What do you think is your mind's reaction to this? It discounts the affirmation. If you continue saying it, your mind just doesn't listen since it asked the question but you didn't hear it or respond. People use many forms of affirmation, thinking they will work, yet they don't. The conflict is that we cannot tell our mind just to change a belief without first releasing the negative attitude and programming held in the database.

The way we set up affirmations is to describe the attitude, concept or feeling *exactly* as it is programmed in your files in the database. Then remove it with the affirmation format described in Chapter 7 of this manual. Once the program and pattern are released, a new file must be created to fill the file folder with a positive program.

There are also many files that can hold programs which also have to be addressed to make sure the program is not recreated and reinstalled. These programs and files can recreate and reinstall the negative file. This format must be followed carefully to make sure the programs are cleared permanently.

There is a difference in how the affirmations will work. If the conflict or affliction is just a belief, all we need to do is clear it with an affirmation. For example, allergies are beliefs with activators and catalysts attached. Find the activator and, with a simple affirmation, it will be cleared permanently. If it is a traumatic experience with an emotional feeling such as rejection attached, then we must locate the block held in the body's cellular memory (in an acupuncture point). When we check, we always ask whether it's a belief or a reality. Reality beliefs and programs are always locked into the body in an acupuncture point, and require specific affirmations that are tailored that specific incident to be cleared.

In working with clients, we have discovered their Conscious Rational Mind is contaminated with false beliefs and attitudes. This is the operating system we use to think with and write programs with. When we hold onto a specific behavior pattern, we can develop a special relationship with these programs, attitudes and beliefs they operate from. This special relationship will become a habit pattern that controls how we function. It will be in denial, operating as an illusion that will block out our awareness of this behavior. We will act out these programs without knowing we are behaving in this way. People observing us will recognize our actions, but we will not. In fact, when people comment about them, we will get defensive and justify our behavior.

An example are people who need validation and attention. They will hijack a conversation and monopolize it, sometimes even speaking over people if they try to cut in on the discussion. If others in the conversation let such person run a monologue and control the discussion, he or she will assume that they have been validated and accepted, since they were not stopped. In actuality, the opposite is true because he or she alienated the other people, even though they didn't protest. We have a double bind here because the objectors did not say anything and the conversation hijacker held an illusion about being validated. Clearing these programs will take some work in tracking down the activator to find where the program is locked in. To release this, we must set up a special affirmation and talk to the Conscious Rational mind with an affirmation similar to the one given in Step 15 of Chapter 10. Most people will not speak their mind about a situation even though it is irritating because they are afraid of rejection an being judged as critical or opinionated so they keep quiet. The interloper walks away feeling he or she was accepted because nobody objected to him or her manipulating the conversation.

Shoulder, back, hip, and joint pain must be addressed with a specific affirmation. We must locate the specific acupuncture point and use a specific affirmation to release blocks in the muscle that are causing the pain. Bones do not create pain. A muscle is putting pressure on a nerve and pinching it, which causes the pain. Muscles can cause bones to put pressure on neuro-pathways by tightening up and putting pressure on what *seems* to be the bones. This happens quite often with back pain. The muscles will tighten down and crunch vertebrae together, creating a curve in the spine known as scoliosis. This will in turn cause sciatic pain. I shrank over an inch in height due to muscle pressure on my spine, which caused a double-S curve in my back and tremendous sciatic pain. I am pain-free now from the releases with the affirmations. Now that my body/mind understands my process, any time I feel pain starting up, I can release it with an affirmation.

When I discovered the cause, we used affirmations, while holding the acupuncture points, to clear all the emotional trauma attached to it. When done this way, pain will be cleared immediately. It can take a while to tap into the incident and develop the ability create affirmations on demand.

In 1984, I was using only four affirmations until a Science of Mind minister made an appointment with me. She said I was limiting myself, and opened my world up to being able to create affirmations for any situation on demand. We now have a basic structure of how to create affirmations which work very well. Enough people have accomplished this for me to assert that anyone can.

Do not feel you must follow the affirmations given in this manual. Let your mind form the affirmations that apply. The patterns listed here are an excellent, proven way to start, and you may find that when you get comfortable with the process in general, you will decide to stay with this general format. After some practice, you will find that you are forming your affirmations as you go.

There is no need to memorize affirmations. This will take some practice and trust in yourself that you can do it. Once you make a win-win situation for yourself by letting yourself open up to the idea that you can do it, they will begin to flow very easy.

Chapter 7

General Pattern for Affirmations

Note: this is *not* the special pattern release we use for multiple incident releases, which is covered below. The general pattern we use for affirmations is a simple four-step affirmation. If you want to work further with affirmations for any purpose, you will find this format to be an effective one for almost all situations. The four steps are done in order to logically satisfy the intellectual mind and to build a strong case for internal support.

The four steps are as follows: ("You" refers to the client.)
1.) Acknowledge who you are;
2.) Acknowledge your creation of a situation;
3.) Release the person, situation or anything else involved; and
4.) Release yourself.

Let's look in more detail at each one of these four steps to see what they are about, why they are included, and where they appear in the process.

1. Acknowledge who you are and claim your power

This step is first because you must call upon your inner powers to direct the energy. If you do not claim your power, you cannot do anything. This is one reason many affirmations do not work. Energy is not power! Power is the ability to command energy while energy is what gets the work done. Depending on the client, we use the phrase, "As the Christ Master self that I am ..." for this part of the affirmation. You may need to adjust the phrasing or the name you invoke if the client was not raised in a Christian family. In this case, use whatever name that puts them in touch with the name of the God presence they were raised under, as that is the name the Middle Self identifies as "power." If you work on an atheist, you can substitute something like, "As the Awakened Powerful Being that I am ..." or something similar.

If in doubt, ask them how they address their most powerful self. After a few sessions, you may find it possible to switch to the current representative of God.

Just be absolutely sure that the entity you are calling on to help is a true ascended Master, and not some guru or impostor. Watch for the Middle Self addressing itself, too.

We have found the process also works with people who claim to be atheists. But, they must have strong convictions of who they are and have some understanding of love as it applies to them. Because we are working with a computer, the mind will accept saying, "I recognize now", or, "I am calling on my Holographic Mind to help me."

We do not put as much emphasis on the preamble as in the past. We have used the affirmations without any phrase to acknowledge the presence of a Source of God within and it seems to work well.

2. Acknowledge your creation of the situation, and release

When you are talking to the Subconscious Mind and it is responding without resistance, we have no problem. The preamble to the affirmation helps clients to claim their personal power. In fact, the mind works like a series of computers, so we can use very short affirmations. There is no need for elaborate, wordy affirmations. All your Subconscious Mind wants to know is:

1.   Are you willing to accept that you participated in the event?
2.   Are you going to release blame and accept that what happened "is what is"?
3.   Are you going to forgive and love the person and/or the event?
4.   Are you willing to accept that you are all right no matter what happened?
5.   Are you going to release and forgive and love yourself?

This is all you need to do release any dysfunction from the body. The body/mind will take care of everything else that is required for healing. We do not use flowery, metaphysical-based affirmations, since we are working with an analog computer that is very linear in its concepts.

When we discovered that the mind backs up all programs daily, it opened a new vista in getting to the cause of why some patterns did not release or were recreated and were back in the file. In 2003, we found that the mind or outside forces can set up activator or recreator viruses which will rewrite a program from a back-up file.

Quite often files may be covered up so they will not be revealed on the first release, and then they will come up later as the computer will fill the empty file space with a program or a pattern that was below it in the file directory.

Many times, we found that we had to go through all the files to release a program. If it was a traumatic experience, each level of the mind may contain the same file. Sometimes the file may be buried in denial or denial-of-denial. To get more understanding of this, read *Your Body Is Talking; Are You Listening?*

One of the major mistakes people make when making affirmation tapes is to record them as if they are saying them to themselves. You can speak in first person when you are reading them to yourself or verbally saying them to yourself. When you record a tape to listen to, you must record it in third person as if you were telling yourself what you want to learn or understand. You must say, "You are doing _____." If use, "I am ____," or, "I have _____." your program manager and file manager will discount the information not allowing the statement to be filed.

When you have decided to change a behavior pattern you have to evaluate the habit or pattern. In creating an affirmation there are three rules that apply to all affirmations:

1.   What are the negatives to the habit/pattern that have created the program and/or file you want to erase and delete? You must describe all the negatives as best as possible in the first part of the affirmation. You will be able to understand this process when you read the affirmations in this manual.

2.   In the middle part of the affirmation, you erase and delete all the negatives by stating, "I accepted these beliefs and attitudes but I know now they are all false and erroneous beliefs, I releasing them now."

3.   Now that all the negatives have been deleted and erased you can put in the positive new program you want to install. It must be done in this form or the affirmation will not work. Stating a bunch of flowery positive statements without releasing the original negative program will not write over the negative patterns. One of the most common ones I have heard is: "I know I am entitled to prosperity and wealth. Money is flowing into my life now." However, your mind is commenting: "Where's the money? When is it going to start flowing into my life?" You keep repeating this affirmation or listening to it. After a time your mind will discount the statement. It may even discount any future affirmations you use if you use the same pattern. The best example of this affirmation is the: "I am entitled to money." (# 25 in this manual.)

Chapter 8

Neuro-Kinesiology

Energy Psychology: Locating the dysfunctional programs with the use of Neuro-Kinesiology (NK).

The Process

My original training in Kinesiology was with Dr. John Diamond, the originator of Behavioral Kinesiology. He had some very unique methods that other practitioners did not use that revealed what the inner mind was holding. His description at the time was that you had to use two hands. Using only the muscle reaction did not give accurate answers. He did not understand at the time why putting his hand over the solar plexus gave a different answer, but it always seemed to be more accurate.

He said, "Do both to check your answer. If the solar plexus answer differs from conventional testing, go with that answer because it will always prove to be the right answer." In my work, I have found this to be true 100% of the time so I do not check with the arm only unless I am demonstrating how the Conscious Mind's answers differ in interpretation. This is not commonly known, and people who use one-arm muscle-testing are working with a process that is only marginally effective.

We have proven that we get accurate answers when you place your hand on the solar plexus when you test. Without connection to the Subconscious Mind's database all we get is interpretations made by the Conscious Mind. Some can be accurate but most are not. The Conscious Mind always wants to be right, safe, secure, and wants to protect you, so all the answers you receive from it are based on those four categories.

Energy Psychology is the process of locating answers so that the dysfunctional programs and patterns can be released. Many modalities claim to fall into Energy Psychology, but we must ask:
- What is the process accomplishing and what are the final results?
- Are results documented over time?
- Did the client obtain the end result being sought?
- Did the condition return at a later date in time or was it cleared completely never to return?

The basic structure of Energy Psychology is the use of affirmations and Kinesiology to release programs and/or beliefs. The first two modalities give us the tools to locate the files in the body/mind. Our mind is a computer and has four operating systems, and we must access the operating system where the files are located to get a correct answer. All Kinesiology modalities use muscle testing to indicate the answers to the questions we are asking. Some methods require you to use specific muscle groups to get answers. All methods except one use the arm or leg only, but this may or may not obtain an accurate answer since you are contacting the Conscious Mind. There is no way to know if the answer is accurate as you are only accessing the Conscious Mind's beliefs.

There are many reasons why the answers obtained may be inaccurate, but we must deal with the issues before we can begin any therapy session or ask questions.

1. Is the polarity balanced?
2. Is the person occupying the body?
3. Are outside forces controlling the answer?
4. Is there a split or multiple personality controlling the mind?
5. Does Inner Conscious Mind have hidden or disguised hidden personality selves?
6. Which one of the mind's operating systems is answering the question?
7. Is the answer a belief or a reality?
8. Is this a true and accurate answer?

Accurate answers originate in or are accessed from Subconscious Mind's database. To accomplish this, we must use one hand over the client's solar plexus. This directly accesses Subconscious Mind and blocks Conscious Mind from providing answers. There are times when we want to connect with Conscious Mind to show the difference in answers as a demonstration.

Part one of the process requires that the person be clear of interference from the mind and from outside forces. We cannot get accurate answers with NK if Conscious Mind interferes. *With NK, you must use one hand over solar plexus to get accurate answers from Subconscious Mind; otherwise you will receive answers from Conscious mind. (We continually stress this critical fact as we do not get accurate answers unless we follow this protocol.)*

This is one of the most important aspects of this process. Most modalities do not use the hand over the abdomen or solar plexus during muscle testing, which means they are only getting the Conscious Mind's viewpoint. The Conscious Mind always wants to be right or may be controlled by outside sources or personality selves. When you find the client's arm is like an iron bar and will not go down with any question or pressure, there is something controlling the client's neurological system. This could turn out to be a muscle battle, but more often it is controlling sub-personalities or entity possession. You will need to clear the entities before you can begin any work.

I developed this process over the last 20 years. I found that I could pick up the answers without any outside means clairvoyantly but many people did not believe what I was telling them, so I developed a system to validate what I was describing in a more definitive manner … and NK is the result. I adapted my training from Behavioral Kinesiology to my new method and we found a new avenue to help people work with questioning, without having to use intuitive or clairvoyant abilities. If we direct the mind to ask the question of the right source, we can access anything, including the Akashic Internet.

There are many ways to use muscle testing, and clarity is of the utmost importance. You can use your mind's awesome abilities to talk to your own body or talk to God with NK just as easily as any other form. You can use any set of muscles that will give you an "up and down" action or an "open/closed" indication. Using fingers, you can hold your thumb and middle finger together and try to pull them apart. Using an arm or a leg, you ask the person to resist your pushing or pulling.

If a sub-personality is in control, you can tap on the thymus gland to regress or progress, or take the person's power down so you can test them. You say, "Reduce available power to 30%," while tapping the thymus gland. (The thymus gland is located behind the collar bone in the chest just below the V-shaped bone below the neck.) Tap on the thymus gland and say to yourself, "Go back to three o'clock this morning." If that does not work, tap again and say, "Reduce the power to 30%." This should work if it is a battle with Middle Self. (Remember to return the client to present time and full power before you finish. If you don't, it could cause problems.) If you are unable to use kinesiology to get accurate answers, it will take someone who is experienced in doing this type of clearing in order to clear the person of outside forces so that you can get accurate answers.

When beginning to work with a client, always set the paradigm so you will know what are *yes* and *no*. First check for strength. Ask the person to resist having their arm to go down. We do not need a muscle battle. Make sure that they do not resist to the point that it will stress their shoulder. *No* will cause a weak reaction no matter how hard they resist. There are exceptions to the case. If there are attached beings present, the arm may react as an iron bar and will not give any indications under any circumstances. At this point, you must go step 6 to clear attached beings.

Generally *yes* is a strong arm and *no* is weak, but some people may respond differently. Ask, "Give me a 'yes' and give me a 'no.'" Test twice to make sure you have the right response. If you have been doing muscle testing for many years, you will have your own protocol that sets the basic parameters before you start so you do not have to do any testing. The client will follow your basic parameters.

In using NK, you use both hands because if you ask a question using the arm only, you will get the belief held in the Conscious Mind, which may not be accurate. Always check to see if the Conscious Mind has a different viewpoint when you begin to do this work so you can experience the difference. To check Subconscious Mind, put one hand over the solar plexus when testing. This will give the Subconscious Mind's viewpoint on the subject. It is always accurate unless you have outside interference. Most forms of Kinesiology suggest you use light pressure. This may work most of the time, but there are occasions when varying pressure must be used due to control by sub-personalities, attached beings or resistance from some program in the mind. It takes practice to recognize all the indications that are presented.

If you begin to test with a person where the arm will not move under questions, make sure you are not having a muscle battle with a strong person. You may have to explain to them this not a competition to see if they can stop you from pushing their arm down. It may take some practice to get the right amount of resistance to let the three minds work with the muscles to get accurate readings.

If the arm will not go down under normal pressure, then you have outside influence. The attached astral beings must be cleared before continuing or you will not get accurate answers. If you notice at times the arm will hold then break and go down, this indicates that the answer would be positive if the person was clear of intervening influences. It may take some work to find the controller, but it must be found or the answers will not be accurate. Sometimes it is a sub-personality but most of the time it is a hidden attached being. (See section on clearing attached beings.)

In all testing, we must make sure polarity is balanced and the person is in their body before any testing can be done. Clients who are not in control of their body/mind will get inaccurate answers.

The tester must be clear of Middle Self control and the need to be right. There are many sub-personalities that will control your ability to use any form of a divination process. The main ones are the Controller, Authority and Manipulator, which always want to be right. An authority figure can manipulate the test results by the mere fact that clients will give their power away to the tester. This is very common in the medical field. Practitioners must be clear also or they will get answers they are looking for if they need to get a desired result and/or answer. If they are selling a product, need to be in control or to validate themselves, and the client has a authority figure program, the client will give their power away to the practitioner without knowing it. As a result, they believe what ever the outcome is right or wrong. This is a great way to sell product because you know that whatever you suggest will be bought because we say it is needed and can prove it with kinesiology. This is not honest but who knows the difference when the tester is not clear themselves. Testers driven by an unclear Conscious Rational Mind that has to be right will not get accurate results. If a person allows the testor to take control over them, they must release their program that gives their power away and reclaim their personal power. Outside forces can also impose controls on the effectiveness of testers, who must be clear of attached beings before they begin sessions, or the beings may jump over to the client.

Back when I did not know that Conscious Rational Mind was the controller, I worked with another therapist with no results because I did not know how to take back control; over CRM.

We also can have interference if the client will not identify with the name they are using. You will need to test for name recognition. If the arm goes weak on using a particular name, test to see which name is causing the difficulty. Quite often, women will have a negative response to their married name if they are divorced or separated from their husband. Sometimes, we can have a negative reaction to a family name if we had a traumatic childhood. Choose a name that tests positive before testing and test again. Sometimes a person will have to change their name as it has so much negative effect on them it causes them to be weak.

If, after considerable testing for name recognition, the tester is unable to test with muscle testing because the arm will not move, there is either a power struggle with Middle Selves' sub-personalities or an outside force. It could be the client does not know how much resistance to put up, or a control sub-personality is trying to control.

Occasionally, we find that Instinctual Mind is controlling. Quite often we find a possessive being has stepped in and taken over and is controlling the muscle test. If this is the case, test for entity attachment and clear cords and entities.

Many clients have an indigenous program that gives away their personal power to authority figures. During childhood, it was an acceptable program so that we would obey our parents, but it has no value as an adult. This must be cleared too. (Process described in "Steps in Sessions.")

Chapter 9

Steps a Practitioner Must Take Before Testing

Steps that must be done prior to testing:

1. *Ground yourself and balance polarity:* This needs to be done only once a day and may be done upon awakening in the morning. This can be done with the wrist holding process as it provides all that is needed. (Process described in "Steps in Sessions")

2. *Do not put shields or energy around yourself to protect yourself.* If you do, you will reflect back all the energy and anything you have removed from the person, stopping the effect of healing.

3. *You must be clear of any attached beings* before beginning a session or you will drop them on a client. Conversely, if you are not protected, clients will drop them on you. One of the major problems we have is passing out in a session caused by entities that will use the client's mind power to knock you out.

4. *Set your paradigm before you begin:* To do this, mentally ask the person to give you a *yes* and a *no*. Most people will respond with a *no* as weak or down. *Yes* will be strong, or up. Using the fingers: closed fingers is usually *yes* and weak or open is *no*. With the finger method you can test yourself. The tester can set whatever paradigm they wish, we prefer *yes* as arm tests strong, *no* as arm can't resist pressure and becomes weak.

5. *Test for name compatibility:* Have the client hold the arm up and test to make sure it holds up against resistance. Ask client to say first and last name while you are holding pressure on the arm. Continue saying the names until the arm gets weak and goes down. This is a test for control by a control/authority sub-personality. You can use this test for either the person being checked or the tester. The most important person to test is the practitioner who is doing the testing. Many times

the tester has received inaccurate answers from me when doing muscle testing me and wondered why. It is because I can control the answers. I know what I am doing but, if the client's sub-personalities are in control, you will not be able to test very effectively. You may want to wait a few minutes and retest to see if Middle self was playing games. If it is, the arm will resist again. Retest again until arm becomes weak. The arm may not go down at all. If this happens, then the person cannot function as a tester and get valid results due to control. You must be in a clear space to do effective muscle testing.

One the most important issues in this training is that a person will attend the workshops then attempt to begin practicing without working on their own issues. We cannot avoid our own issues, yet we have found that more than 50% of the attendees will not get into recovery. Therapists must be working on their own issues regularly with another therapist; practitioners must be in recovery working with their own issues all the time. N/CR brings them up and will interfere with the process when working with a client. If you do not want to work with your own issues when they come up with a client, you will slide the client out of the tight space you put yourself in. You may even pass out during the session if you do not want to face the issue. This can happen to both the client and the practitioner. Sometimes it can happen simultaneously.

Chapter 10

Steps in N/CR Sessions

Each one of the following steps is to clear an aspect of the mind of programs and beliefs that we have accepted as our general operating modality. Quite often we find that people will resist, and contend that nothing is wrong with them and we are going too far. If this happens, the changes are threatening a part of their mind.

After we clear all the programs in this level then we go to the next phase—Energy Medicine, which is part two of the process and where we begin releasing programs from the cellular memory from the body.

Each time an emotional reaction is recorded, it also deposits in the body at specific points in the various muscle groups throughout the body. Traumatic experiences will have a major reaction in the body. (This is process is described in *Your Body Is Talking; Are You Listening?* published by Personal Transformation Press, and available from amazon.com, barnesandnoble.com, Barnes & Noble and Borders book stores, plus many local book stores [ISBN 1-891962-01-9])

Note: The following steps must be done in order. You must know what you are doing, so do not attempt to do this work without reading the descriptions first. Each one applies to a particular aspect of Energy Psychology and Energy Medicine. If clients' emotions come up in any release pattern, tell them to let it out and not to suppress it. The emotion is programmed and locked into the body's cellular memory, so in the Energy Medicine phase, we will find out why the emotion came up and release the program.

Step 1: Check for polarity balance

Using NK when you check for polarity, if the arm goes down, polarity is reversed. A strong arm may indicate it is balanced. Check the client for being in the body, and then for attached beings. If the arm is extremely strong on all three and all of them indicate *yes*, you may have to clear entities before going any further. (Go to step 3 for process.) If polarity is reversed, a *no* will record as a *yes* and conversely. Restoring polarity can be done using an ancient Chinese balancing method or auricular zero point stimulation:

Show the client how to put wrists together and hold arms. Hold the insides of your wrists together, with your fingers pointing toward your elbows, one on top and one under. It makes no difference which way they are positioned, on top or bottom. The lines on your wrists at the base of your palm must be aligned, touching flat together or it will not work. There is an offset step on the base of each palm. Push those together so the bracelet lines on each wrist are touching. Then place your hands with your fingers grasping your forearms, pointing toward your elbows just above the wrists. Hold for two to ten minutes. For best results, hold for five to ten minutes a day. You will feel your wrist begin to pulse or become warm. Hold until pulsing stops.

This polarity exercise will balance all your electromagnetic fields, your quadrant energies and the electrical flow in the meridians. It will also balance all your chakras and ground you at the same time. Remember that this will not work if the circulation meridian is not connected. The circulation meridian stops at the end of your third or middle finger. When you connect the meridians by holding them together, you complete the circuit so it creates a circular flow of energy around the body. Many people have a hard time understanding the positions without a diagram, so carefully explain and show the position to the client.

Sometimes we can encounter a blowout on one side of body, due to a polarity reversal caused by a birth trauma (or a switch of plans before birth) where the soul changed the path and chose different parents than were originally intended. The soul takes over a body that would have been stillborn as the original soul changed its plans and vacated before birth. This can be corrected by using an affirmation asking File and Program Manager to erase and delete the file and install a new file to correct the polarity balance.

Note: This exercise must be done everyday. Repeat everyday without fail to insure your body is in polarity!

Step 2: Check to see if client is in the body

Using NK, check for the client walking out of body. (*Strong* indicates in body; *weak* is out of body) To pull a person back into his body, use the following affirmation.

Ask the client to repeat after you:

"This is (month, day and year). I am____ [first name] _____ [last name], I am in my conscious, rational, decision-making mind. I fully occupy this body."

This affirmation will always pull a person solidly back in. You may have to use this during the session, too. Remind them to use this affirmation every day when they are doing the balancing exercise in the morning. Quite often these tests bring up resistance, fear or insecurity. This may cause a person to go out of their body. We can check for this when the arm goes weak. To get back in, we must call their name and ask Higher Self to bring them back in their body.

If not successful, use the following:

If you have a mushy muscle response after they say the affirmation, check to see if they want to be here. There could be fear of having to deal with issues, which will cause a client to block themselves by losing connection or "graying out." Check for *Instinctual Mind* control. You may have to release that before going any further. You may have to use the affirmation to get them back into their body again. Always finish with the affirmation above.

Many people are *graying out* or *browning out*. They can function but only at survival level. They need to recognize when they are walking out and say this affirmation; it may be needed 10 or 20 times a day. During a session, if the mind does not want to deal with an issue, it will black a person out. They may appear as if they are going to sleep, but they are passing out due to mind control, so you must bring them back into the body. Wake them up and ask Higher Self to bring them back into the body. This may need to be done numerous times. More and more people are walking out and not knowing it until they are reminded of how it feels.

Another cause is that a person's name can throw them out of the body. This happens quite often with divorced women, so after a divorce, women should always return to their given name. We have had instances where either the given name *and* the divorced name will throw a person out of their body. It can happen to men, but not very often.

Step 3: Check for Split or Multiple Personalities

We have discovered this is one of the most important aspects of this work and is very critical since over 99% of our clients have them. Many people do not want to acknowledge or even believe in this concept, but it is one of the most critical steps in the clearing process. We have even had clients say, "No one can control my life," which is not true when you understand this concept. We have no defense from them as they took over when we walked out and gave up control.

We did not discover how critical this is to the treatment process until April, 2003. This is the answer to the majority of the dysfunctional behavior, illness, disease, and lack of self-esteem, self-worth, self-confidence and success in most people's lives. We have seen miracles happen when we clear the separation from self so the true or real self can get back in control of the person's life.

Split and multiple personalities must use totally separate operating systems which will control the mind. We must get back to true self to begin healing.

Most people do not want to even consider this as a possibility. This is true if a separated self is running your life. It is not going to let you destroy it, so it will fight for control. Many times when working with clients, this has happened with me. We do not make any progress or they will avoid coming to see me and they do not know why. These separated selves will create fear or try to stop clients from recognizing that they are being controlled. This explains why people would see me once and never come back. In fact, they would avoid me, not return calls and miss appointments because the date would be erased from their mind. It is very hard to keep a schedule when this happens. Now that we have the opportunity to clear all these saboteurs, we are finding that people can keep their goals and appointments and stay on the path with their intentions, commitments and goals.

I always wondered why people would not make appointments when I had clearly demonstrated with them at a lecture that they had specific issues that must be released. Many times people would see me for one session and never come back, or they would not show up for an appointment and never call back. When I talked with them later, they could not recall making an appointment. This explains why this step is so vital in treatment process.

Some people may describe this as splintering or separation from soul and/or spirit, but that is not my perception at all. Our spirit and soul are observing us all the time, wondering when we are going take responsibility and come back to our true self. They know what has happened to us but are powerless to clear the separation unless we can listen to them. If we are blocked and allowing a disowned or false self to run our life, we have no opportunity to get in contact with who we are.

In the past, we overlooked this aspect of the mind because we did not want to get into mental illness or even suggest that it could exist in people who did not have obvious characteristic behavior patterns of mental imbalance. We must clear them, as they are usually in control of the person's mind. Quite often, we have found that just clearing them will eliminate a disease or illness on the spot.

During 2004, many aspects of the mind were presented to us in sessions where we had to deal with a new concept. We had to take stock of why we were missing these parts of the mind and why they have been eluding us. We found the cause with the discovery of split and/or multiple personalities. In psychology, this is not a common experience unless a person has mental dysfunction. We seldom checked for split personalities in the past, assuming that if a person did not display mental conflicts with personality identification difficulties, they did not have split or multiple personality conflicts. It is quite obvious when people have mental disability problems, so we only checked people that had obvious mental/behavior conflicts for split personalities.

It seems now that we overlooked some very important aspects of the mind because we did not know about them. Since this was brought to my attention, we have done a considerable amount of research to find out why they had eluded us. They take on separate identities with different habit patterns. Sometimes our mind will assign and take on different names to identify itself. We did not realize there are disguised subtle forms of split or multiple personalities that hide behind personality selves and artificial intelligence in Inner Conscious Mind.

The entry point is during the time when a child is in Magical Child Syndrome. (It doesn't seem to make any difference if it was the positive side or negative side.) They were created when a person goes into Magical Child looking for playmates or escaping from fear and abuse. If a child is feeling rejected and abandoned or looking for playmates due to loneliness and stays in Magical Child for any length of time, the split personality can be created. The longer one spends in Magical Child, the more likely it is that multiple or split personalities will be created.

We have found that most of the time they are hidden under some other file name or have created a name for themselves that blocks our ability to locate them. The way we identify them is through aberrational behavior patterns or inability to stay in control of their life, disorientation, indecision, procrastination, invalidator programs, or unable to set or meet goals.

Many times they may be hidden and not functioning unless the crisis that created them is being confronted or the catalyst is triggered. In this case we must use the right words to identify the split personality or multiple personalities. We have found that people who function from split personalities are not able to identify with their true self. They act out in ways that give an impression of who they appear to be, but it is an illusion created by the split personality. If the personality self has taken over, it pushes true self to the background where it has no control over the person's life.

Quite often we would identify a person as a controller/manipulator, yet in reality they are scared and afraid of rejection, so they hold on and cling to what appears to be control. In actuality, they cling to their partner or anyone out of fear of being rejected and abandoned, trying to control so they will not lose their support. When we remove the split personality and empower them to take responsibility and control of their life, they can recognize they were operating from fear of loss. True self would not act out in a controlling manner. With this observation, we can assume that all people who are controller, manipulator, authority figures are functioning from personality selves, and not true self.

Another aspect we found was that many times these personality selves carry a disease or illness syndrome that is not in the true self's files so the disease is controlled and created by the false self, personality self, split or multiple personality. When we clear the files controlling the personality selves who are manifesting through the disease or illness, the symptoms will abate and disappear. This has been documented on a TV special where a woman had a brain tumor. When she went back to the doctor the following week for a pre-op examination, the tumor was gone. He called the psychiatrist she was seeing, to validate that she was multiple personality. One personality had the tumor; the other did not. This obvious situation proves that all diseases are controlled by the mind. Each personality self has a separate set of operating programs and systems to meet its own needs.

Different people have differing resistance levels that will cause split personalities to activate. A small crisis will drive some people into a split personality whereas other people have the ability, with considerable strength, to avoid such traumatic experiences. It all depends on a person's capability to withstand stress and conflict and handle themselves. People who have had a traumatic experience that created a split personality may be strong enough to prevent it from controlling them most of the time.

The only difference between mental dysfunction such as bipolar (manic depressive) and a seemingly normal person is the *interpretation* of their position in life. Victims are subject to mental dysfunction whereas survivors view life as a challenge and can control most dysfunctional behavior most of the time even though it continues to manifest occasionally.

The third situation are children who are abused and/or feel as if they have no support, help, validation and love from their parents. Dark forces prey on them and can take them over when they are hiding in the split personalities. Many times they grow up with this attachment which does not act out until they are adults. Recognizing this form of split personality is hard, as it is very subtle and covert. Sometimes personalities will sit in the background and sabotage the person so it appears that it is a behavior pattern over which the person has no control. Since they are not aware of the habit pattern, they will deny and defend their behavior. To the outsider, the defense is obvious and defeating, but when one is in it, he cannot recognize it.

If it is a disowned self, we must bring it into ourselves so we can make peace with it and learn the lesson from it. The false self was created by us to avoid emotional trauma, so we must release and forgive ourselves for creating an escape hatch from reality to avoid pain and trauma. We are beginning to understand now many forms of escape, which all have payoffs to get a desired result.

Most of the time we find the split personality that was taken over by a possessive being was able to come in as a magical playmate. As children, we cannot to tell the difference between magical illusions our mind creates and actual possessive beings who come in masquerading as magical playmates. When we are children, they can walk in without any resistance. They will disguise or cloak themselves so we cannot identify them. When they are hidden under personality selves, we must ask the right questions or we will not be able to identify them.

One split personality will have a name. If there is more than one split personality, identify its number and insert the split personalities with the client's name in the second line of the affirmation. Insert the number of multiple personalities in third line. Recite the following affirmation to clear the split personalities and multiple personalities.

You may find more named split personalities in future sessions. Every time a client walks out due to trauma, their mind may create more named split personalities; we have found up to four. This is the reason for dysfunctional behavior in mental patients. These personality selves are fighting for control and, depending on the trigger or program that activates each personality self, they will determine which one is in control. In the average client, one will take over control and suppress the others so there is no noticeable dysfunctional behavior.

The release affirmation follows these questions. There will not be any resistance as we are working with a computer operating system. We can delete and erase their control by simply removing the operating system they function under.

"Are there any split and multiple personalities cloaked, disguised, hidden in underground files or operating under a different name from your given name in Conscious or Subconscious Mind?"

If yes, ask: "Are they identified by the person's given name?"

If no, ask: "Is it an English given name?"

If not, ask: "What language is it in?"

Check for beginning letter of name: "Is it A to G, H to L, M to R, S to Z?"

After you have established the beginning letter, go through a series of names with this letter. Quite often, the name will come to you intuitively.

Use the affirmation on the next page to clear the personalities:

Affirmation to release split and multiple personalities:

"I am asking you, file and program managers, to remove _____, ____ split personalities, ____ multiple personalities, and _____ altered or disguised personality selves.

"Put them in the trash bin. Delete, erase and destroy all their operating programs, patterns and systems and operating instructions from Conscious Mind's, Middle Self's, and Subconscious Mind's operating files, back-up files, past, present, current, future time-line files, denial, and denial-of-denial files, history archive files in the Subconscious Mind, all unmarked, mismatched files, mislabeled, untitled files, orphan files, forgotten files, ghost files, neglected files and all restricted files that have been prohibited, forbidden, distorted, aborted, damaged, and locked up as unavailable or rendered unopenable.

"Put them in the trash bin. Remove all the recreator, reactivator, regenerator, reconstructor, reproducer and reinstaller virus files. Lock them up and put them in the trash bin so they will never affect me again. I am asking you to clear the trash bin. Empty and delete all files, send them to the incinerator and burn them now. I am loving and forgiving myself now."

Step 4: Set up the Trash Bin and Incinerator

Before we can delete and clear any programs, we must set up a receptacle to deposit deleted and erased files, programs and directories. In the normal course of daily activities, our mind deposits unused and deleted programs in the recycle bin and the archives. When we want to delete a specific program or file, we must put it in the trash bin.

Affirmation to create trash bin and incinerator:

"I am asking file and program managers to establish a trash bin with incinerator to destroy all deleted files and information. Install these programs in Conscious Mind, Subconscious Mind, history archives, and all operating systems now. Send all deleted programs files, programs and operating systems to the trash bin immediately. Empty the trash bin daily, sending all files to the incinerator. Thank you for your help."

Step 5 Removing Cords

We can get cords attached to us from anyone who can get close enough if they are controllers or they want to drain our energy. Sometimes a relationship breaks up but one of the parties does not want to let go, and may cord the former partner. Low energy people may cord higher energy people to drain their energy.

- If this tests as *yes*, then check for locations: forehead (third eye), throat, solar plexus, base of spine, and brain stem (back of the neck).
- Use your *etheric* fingers (invisible extensions to each of your fingers) to grab them and twist and pull them out from each location.
- Command that beings leave and give them 15 seconds; if they do not leave, clap attached beings out in the same manner as before.
- Check again to make sure they have been removed.
- When they are clear, you can resume the process.

Step 6: Make peace with Middle Self, Ego, and Program and File Managers

Before you can change any programs, we must make peace with Middle Self and take your power back from it. We must make friends with ego and forgive ourselves for beating it up. Ask if Middle Self and file manager will work with you. Seldom will we get a *yes* to the question unless a person has done extensive work and has been successful in reprogramming the mind.

Few methods and processes available will be successful in actually reprogramming the mind, since they do not first get support from both Middle Self and ego. Middle Self is the program manager and must work with you to coordinate program installation. In most cases, it was handling writing the programs and installing them. We must take that responsibility back and reclaim our personal power. (This is the primary concept in my books).

Ego is the file manager that files and retrieves programs in your Subconscious Mind. If it is not working for you, it will not file any programs or affirmations in Subconscious Mind. The programs will have to pass through Middle Self's censor program. If it chooses not to let the file through, affirmations will not work in most cases. If Middle Self is left to run on its own program, file manager and ego will only install files from the information that Middle Self approves. This may include negative affirmations that reinforce existing dysfunctional programs. Middle Self will not give up control since it has been appointed as your protector unless you rewrite its operating system. Ego will not allow programs or files to be installed if it feels that you are attacking it. It will shut down and little will get past it. Since it is your memory retrieval system, it must be functioning properly.

Since both program manager and file manager are operating systems, their operating protocol can be rewritten and reinstalled with the proper operating programs.

The following affirmations will rewrite the operating systems and the protocol under which Middle Self and ego operate. Once they cooperate with you, they will file or edit any program you want them to. First, ask:

"Are file manager and program manager working now?"

If not, we must use the affirmation below before reprogramming is possible. I am finding now that quite often a person will return for a session and we find that file and program manager programs are not working. Before reinstalling, have client read the first paragraph of the Instinctual Mind file affirmation, then test again. If they went into survival, it was crashed and will be reactivated after reading the Instinctual Mind affirmation.

Affirmation to make peace and reinstall file and program manager:

"In accordance with universal law, free will and the law of right action, I recognize now that I must make peace with my Middle Self. I am doing that now. I know that you are the program manager and you do the best you can with the programs you have available. It is my responsibility to reclaim my personal power. I want you to know, Middle Self, that I am taking my power back now. I am not taking your power. I am only taking back the power that is rightly mine. I have no intention of damaging or destroying you because you are an important part of my team and I need your help. I know now I must be the chief computer operator and the program supervisor. It is my responsibility to install all the program files now. I am asking you to refrain from making judgments and creating sub-personalities and programs. I reserve the right to rewrite any file in keeping with my highest good. I thank you for your help. I am grateful we are now a team.

"I must make peace with my ego now. Due to false information, misconception, and misinterpretation, I felt you were the villain and the enemy. I recognize my mistake now. I know now that you are the file manager, secretary and librarian for my Subconscious Mind computers. I know as the file manager you do the best you can with the programs you have available to you. I am committed to making friends

with you now. I am giving myself 100% permission to forgive myself for any harm and trauma that I may have inflicted on you in the past based on my misconception of what your role in my life is. I am asking for your forgiveness. I need your help since you are an important part of my team. I am grateful we can now work as a team. I am forgiving any errors, misconceptions or misinterpretations I held about your behavior. I am accepting and loving you. I am loving and forgiving myself. I am installing these operating systems in the file now. I thank you for your help. I am loving and forgiving myself for abdicating my personal power, and I am doing that now."

Step 7: Instinctual Mind Survival Programs

In the past, I assumed that only people who had serious or life-threatening illnesses had Instinctual Mind activated. We did not check everyone for instinctual files. We would not suspect them to have them activated in the average person. In the past we found the Instinctual Mind activated only in people with major traumatic experiences and life threatening illnesses. Now it seems that they are activated in everyone who feels any of the above fear feelings or has sub-personalities installed that support the client's refusal to take responsibility. The sub-personality seems to take over after it is installed.

Another aspect we have discovered is that if we remove all the back-up files that allow us to escape to avoid responsibility, fear, abuse and pain, the Instinctual Mind will be activated. If it is able to take control over 70% or more of the mind, it will begin to block out many constructive files. It will block out the love program, file manager, program manager, and activate many disorientation and confusion sub-personalities. When a person is confronted with issues they do not want to deal with on a subconscious level, they will go into survival, giving their power up as it takes over 100% control of the mind through Inner Conscious Mind. It blanks all files on the hard disk as the person goes into total survival. The more control you give up, the more it takes over. I have just begun checking for Instinctual Mind control and *I want to die* programs as I began to find they were activated in many people.

In the fall of 2000, Instinctual Mind files began to show up in a few people who did not have life-threatening diseases, as the stress level in society builds up, the pressure shifts, and time speeds up, all leading to the critical mass shift. Following the events of September 11, 2001, it began to affect everyone. We discovered that Instinctual Mind was being activated by survival self as people retreated into survival mode. The file was activated by feelings of frustration, indecision, futility and lack of direction because of how unsettled people were feeling. They created *I want to die* programs and *fear of dying* programs because their mind could not deal with all conflicts. Now 99% of the clients tested have this program activated, making this probably the most critical of the dysfunctional programs we are finding now.

Clients who have had traumatic experiences in childhood have often had this problem most of their lives, but we could not understand the cause. Clearing and uninstalling the Instinctual Mind and erasing the operating system cleared the *I want to die* and *fear of dying* programs, and many of the malfunctions cleared up. If clients feel futility, frustrated, indecision, loss of direction, the Instinctual Mind program will automatically be installed. Most of the time *I want to die* and *fear of dying* programs will get installed also. If both of them are installed you will have to check for *Alzheimer's* programs as they may also be installed. After testing, many clients, we identified this combination as the cause for Alzheimer's disease.

If the person does not know it is activated, it will eventually destroy him and he will die or go into regression with Alzheimer's disease.

(Instinctual Mind itself cannot be destroyed as it is an indigenous program. It has to be locked up in the archives.)

This affirmation must be used for *fear of dying, I want to die* and *Alzheimer's* programs. Begin by asking:

"Are any instinctual mind files active?"
"Are any fear of dying programs active?"
"Are any Alzheimer's programs active?"
"Are I want to die programs active?"

Important Note: In this and all other affirmations, "Infinity number of programs" (or sub-personalities) will remove any number that are present. It must be "an infinity number," not "an infinite number," to work.)

Affirmation to release Instinctual Mind file, Survival and Alzheimer's programs:

"In accordance with universal laws of free choice and right action, I am asking my Higher Self, file and program manager to access all files, capture, quarantine and remove the Instinctual Mind's operating files and the survival program from Conscious Mind, Inner Conscious Mind, Middle Self, Subconscious Mind's operating files and history archive files, past, present, current, future and parallel time-line files, denial, and no perception of denial-of-denial files. Remove reinstaller, reactivator, recreator and regenerator virus programs. *Uninstall the operating system* and the interface it operates from and lock them in the history section. Delete, erase and destroy all the programs, patterns, records, operating programs, and operating instructions. Lock them up so they will never affect me or recreate again and put them in the trash bin.

"I am asking Higher Self, File and Program Manager to remove all the following programs:
- *An infinity number* of survival programs
- *An Infinity number* of I want to die programs.
- *An Infinity number* of fear of dying programs.
- *An infinity number* of Alzheimer's memory failure programs.

"Put them in the trash bin. Delete, erase and destroy all their operating instructions, operating systems and operating programs, patterns, programs and records. Put them in the trash bin, delete, burn and incinerate all files. I thank you for your help. I am loving and forgiving myself now."

Step 8: Install the Love Program to Receive Love

"Receiving Love" is one of the most critical programs of all. Seven out of ten people are rejected before they are born. Can the person receive love and love themselves? We find very few people are able to love themselves and receive love. Over the last 25 years, we have found that 95% of the population is unable to love themselves or receive love. When checking for these programs, check to see whether the mother wanted children, and whether the mother wanted that particular child.

Since I began checking for the love program, the statistics have changed. I was not going into the files very deeply at first, so my feedback was that two in five (40%) clients were rejected between birth and five years old. Now it has gone up to nine out of ten (90%). We can go months or even years before we find a client who actually loves him/herself. It is increasingly so with children under ten years old, even though there seems to be a resurgence among some young parents to provide a loving environment for their children. The cause is the default program we accepted from our parents on raising children.

Check for love without putting hand on the solar plexus first, as this will demonstrate how the Conscious Mind feels about love. Normally this will test strong if there is a file in the Conscious Mind. If it tests weak, there is no file installed on love. If the first test is positive, then test by putting your hand over the solar plexus and test again. If this tests positive, sometimes a person may check strong on loving self when it is an illusion, because they have been working on loving themselves for years. They have convinced themselves that they love themselves to the point they will test strong for loving themselves.

If you suspect that this is not true, ask if this is a belief or a reality. You must have all files open to do so. Check denial files, and no perception of denial, which may reveal that the first test may be inaccurate. Only 1 in 5,000 people we have worked with can love themselves and receive love without limitations. This is a tragic but true statistic.

Remember that this program will not lock the love affirmation into the file unless you first release the actual rejection programs that are located in the cellular memory acupuncture points on the body on the left side, near the top of the shoulder blade. There many more *rejection, I am not all right, I do not fit in, nobody wants me, I am not accepted, nobody loves me, and I have no right to live* programs located in the same area if the person was rejected before they were born or as a young child.

Test first without putting hand on abdomen. This must be done first to establish if there is a file in the data base. Ask,

"Are you loving yourself?"

If test is weak, there is no love program in the file. The hard disk file on love does not exist. If the test is strong, continue testing with hand on solar plexus. Ask:

"Is there an operational love file? Are you loving yourself? Are you able and willing to receive love?"

If either one of these test weak, the program has been written over. It is not operating, the original must be uninstalled and a new program installed. Use the following affirmation for this purpose.

Affirmation to reinstall Love program:

"In accordance with universal law of free choice, and right action, I now recognize that love is my responsibility. I know now and accept that I am entitled to unconditional love. I know that love is kindness, caring, acceptance without judgment and control, acceptance without manipulation and authority. I accept that now. I am now removing all overshadows that block me off from God and I am doing that now. I know that I can reestablish the presence of God in my life now. I am doing that now. I am now removing all inner shadows that block me off from my Higher Self. I know now that I am entitled to live in peace, happiness, harmony and joy. I accept that now. I am loving and forgiving my mother and father for being unable to provide me the love model and the unconditional love I was entitled to. I am loving myself and forgiving myself and I am doing that now."

When you install the love program, you can ask why the love program was lost. Use NK to ask the following questions:

1. **Did your mother want children?**
2. **Were you rejected before you were born?**
3. **Did she want you as a child?**
4. **Did she accept you after you were born?**
5. **Did she accept you at anytime in your childhood?**

If the client was not rejected before they were born, follow with these questions:

1. **Did you bond with your mother after birth?**
2. **Were you rejected between birth and five years old?**
3. **Were you rejected from six to ten?**

Continue until you find the exact year by narrowing it down in five year time frames as above. Then go to one year segments until you locate the exact year. This usually coincides with the year Magical Child Syndrome was activated.

Situations with the father will not normally appear until about five to seven years of age, unless the mother abandons the child and the father has to step in and take over. If this happens, we have issues with competition between child and mother for father's attention. In this case, the mother would be an adult child.

Step 9 Remove Medical Model and Skeptic and Doubter Sub-personalities

The average person will accept the medical model as a general valid pointer as to how one should deal with medical emergencies, illness, disease, and most dysfunctional behavior. The more one is caught in or believes that medical science and the practitioners of allopathic medicine have the answers to illness and disease, the more skeptical a person will be of alternative practices. At the conscious level, we may not agree or be aware that we have accepted this concept as a working program in our mind. We may agree with and partake in alternative practices, yet if a sub-personality exists in the mind, a person may be a doubter of anything he/she believes or has had direct experience with. Even if one does accept and use alternative practices and these sub-personalities are operational programs, we will be in a double bind. Under crisis situations where we are in a survival or autopilot situation, we will go the conventional medical route, even if we oppose the concept.

Programs that can be released with a simple affirmation may encounter opposition, such as allergy or illness programs that are caused by a diagnosis or belief created by an authority figure. Catalysts, triggers, and activators can also block release of programs. If the program has no basis in actual reality (i.e., a belief), we must check for opposition.

Any Skeptic or Doubter sub-personalities or unbelief programs operating will reinstall any program our mind considers operational.

Ask whether any of these programs are operating:

1. **Skeptic**
2. **Doubter**
3. **Medical model**
4. **Cultural model**
5. **Religious model**
6. **Societal models**
7. **Lack of faith, trust, belief, acceptance and/or lack of self-respect**

Use the following affirmation on the next page to remove and delete them.

Affirmation to remove models, Skeptic, Doubter:

"In accordance with universal law of free choice, I am asking My Higher Self, File and Program Manager to capture, quarantine and remove:

- *An infinity number* of Skeptical sub-personalities and put them in the trash bin.
- *An infinity number* of Doubter sub-personalities and put them in the trash bin.
- *An infinity number* of Medical models and put them in the trash bin.
- *An infinity number* of Religious models and put them in the trash bin.
- *An Infinity number* of Cultural models and put them in the trash bin
- *An Infinity number* of Society models and put them in the trash bin.
- *An Infinity number* of lack of faith, trust, belief, acceptance and lack of self respect put them in the trash bin.

Uninstall the operating systems. Delete, erase and destroy all programs, patterns, records, operating instructions, operating programs and operating systems. Lock them up and send them to the trash bin so they will never affect me again. Burn and incinerate all files now. Thank you for your help. I am loving myself and forgiving myself now."

Step 10 Remove Inner Conscious Mind's Control.

Over the years, we have been restoring control by removing the Magical Child Syndrome and Inner Child, bringing stability to clients' lives. We did not recognize that we were only setting up an illusion of stability, because we were not addressing the end result of how our mind ends up on autopilot, with artificial intelligence running our life in the first place. Since we did not totally clear out and reprogram how the major players in our Conscious Mind set up the operating systems, most of the time people fall right back into survival when they had to deal with a confrontational situation.

Recently we have discovered that when clients are confronted with a major conflict, feel threatened or end up in a indecisive situation that causes them to become disassociated or disoriented in their mind and/or is causing them to fall back into survival, they sometimes escape into Magical Child, and Inner Conscious Mind takes over. When this happens, program and file managers are disabled and quite often the Love program is disabled or crashed. When we go through the Instinctual Mind program and release it again, file and program managers are restored and sometimes the Love program is restored. Sometimes the Love program is destroyed and has to be reinstalled. When this happens, it is like your computer going into "safe mode" so you can diagnose the problem and correct it. Unfortunately, the human mind does not have a program that signals us that we have gone into survival. If you are sensitive to your feelings and can recognize that your operational modality has shifted, you can remedy the situation. But, most people do not recognize as they go on autopilot and shut down their sensing ability. As a result of these blocking programs, most people are operating from survival.

Inner Conscious Mind is where artificial intelligence, Instinctual Mind files, Magical Child, autopilot, Inner Child, Critical Parent, and shadow selves operate from. All these operating systems are in Middle Self, but it does not have any control over the processing once it creates an operating program. If sub-personalities are running your life, you are not thinking with Conscious Mind. Inner Conscious Mind and personality self are running the show. In the past, we used to remove all of them but left the operating system intact so they can recreate very easy. Unless we remove them along with all the other programs, recreator, reactivator, regenerator, reconstructor and reinstaller programs exist in the backup-files.

If Inner Conscious Mind and/or personality selves have control, it may not want to give it up. If you have tried to get your life on track over a period of time and have not succeeded, then either Inner Conscious Mind and/or personality selves have control and will hold on. You may think that your life is running well, as there are not too many incidences of situations not working. But if indecision, disorientation, procrastination, feeling confused, frustrated, out of sorts, not being accepted or validated, or illness keeps plaguing you, you can be sure that either Inner Conscious Mind and/or personality selves have some effect on the feelings or situations. It can hit, and then back away if you get a handle on your situation, which can make you feel as if you're over the effects that hit you, but this does not clear its control as the programs continue to be active in the background. They have let you take control until you reach another confrontation or crisis situation. When we confront Inner Conscious Mind's control, it can cause you to react without control, to get sick, or to feel upset, so you want to get away from this conflict or become depressed. They are all fronts that Inner Conscious Mind can stop you from reclaiming your personal power and taking control back. We must remove the personality selves' operating systems from Conscious Mind. It can hold onto files that will block us from releasing beliefs that are not real but it feels it needs for security and safety.

This affirmation is two in one, for personality selves and Inner Conscious Mind. The Personality Selves are the aspect of ourselves that creates separation from true self, and the aspect of ourselves that practitioners describe as the splintered or fractured soul or spirit. Some people have described this as "our spirit going away from us," so we must recover it, too. In our research, we have found that none of this has any connection with soul or spirit. Our mind can play mind games with us, letting us think we are recovering something. It is all an illusion because we think something is happening, yet it is our mind letting us feel that we are recovering our soul or spirit, when in fact our soul and spirit are watching this charade wondering why we are trying to rescue them when they have all the answers if we would only listen to their direction.

Deleting the operating systems and bringing ourselves back to true reality opens a Pandora's Box, as all the doors are open and the light shines in to illuminate our true being. It can cause crashes in our reality and throw us back into survival if we do not take care to watch every action and response we take or are involved in. With the following affirmation, we are declaring that we will take control of our mind so we must follow the directions we are stating. We will be tested to see if we can handle the temptations or fall back and escape responsibility. Any conflict within ourselves can cause us to stumble and fall back and lose control.

If personality self will not let go or clear, check for retreating into survival. We must check ourselves to make sure we have not fallen back if we are confronted with a conflict, indecision, disorientation, confusion or loss of control. We can check for survival with NK or a pendulum for answers. If a client has retreated into survival, check for file and program manager. If they test negative, check for the Love file. If it is crashed too, then we are in survival. If this is a second session, have the client recite the Reclaim Personal Power affirmation in Step 14. Check again for the Love program and file manager. They should be up and working again. If not, have the client recite them again.

Then go to split personalities. You must clear the hiding places for the personality selves before you can release them.

This is a long affirmation that I once felt had to be tailored to each person's situation but I have found that this is not required. Since Inner Middle Self is controlled by programs, this affirmation will break down its control, rewriting and reprogram it so you can reclaim control over your life. In step 11, we delete it so that it cannot be reinstalled.

This is the ultimate take responsibility affirmation. If you fall back into survival too many times, you may find that you are going to have a battle with your inner selves to get control back. You must be very careful with how you interpret your feelings and how thoughts manifest. Also be careful how you feel about what others say to you and their actions toward you. If you give up your power and control in a crisis situation, and go into survival, Inner Conscious Controlling Mind will be forced to take over. Any of these can be programming and cause you to fall back.

To find out if Inner Conscious Mind and personality self will cooperate, ask:

1.   Will Inner Conscious Mind cooperate with reclaiming your personal power?
2.   Will the personality self release control over your Conscious Mind?
3.   How much control do you have over your life right now, on a scale from 0 to 100?
4.   What is the self-esteem/self-worth value on a scale from 0 to 100?
5.   What is the endocrine operational function percentage on a scale from 0 to 100?
6.   What is Immune System operational function percentage on a scale from 0 to 100?
7.   What is the body's operational frequency? (The body's operational frequency should be between 15-25 hertz (Hz) but can be up to 3300 Hz.)

If the client's adrenal function is down to 25%, they are entering clinical depression. As a result, body function could be shut down at anytime. When you are in 100% control of your life, with no conflicts to adversely affect your adrenal function, it will return to normal. When the adrenal glands are overworked, it leads to depression. (See StressBuster in Appendix for solution.)

Affirmation to release Inner Conscious Mind and personality selves:

"In accordance with universal law of free choice and right action, I am asking my Inner Conscious Mind Personality Selves to work with me now. I realize that I gave my power away, letting you, autopilot and artificial intelligence take over to escape from fear and trauma. I am ready and willing to face it now. I am committed to taking responsibility and reclaiming my personal power now. I know I must take control over my life now. I am committed to reclaiming my personal power now. I am asking you, Inner Conscious Mind, personality selves to work with me. I know I gave up my personal power, responsibility and control in the past and let autopilot take over my life. I appreciate that you were able to help me survive and handle my life. I know now that it is my responsibility to take control back now. It is now my intention to reclaim my personal power to take responsibility to work through my issues. I am making a 100% commitment to discipline and take control over my life now. I recognize that I have done this before and you have had to go in and pick up the pieces because I backed out and ran out on my responsibility. This will not happen again. I am committed to take responsibility and follow through with my commitment now. You may not believe me because you have had to take over before when I vacated my control in the past, but I am committed to follow through this time without fail. I will not let you down this time, as I know I must follow through and take control of my life now. I know I have let you run my life for many years, but I was not aware that I avoided taking responsibility in the past. I know now that I cannot continue with this behavior any longer. I am in total agreement that I must take back my power now and I am doing that now. I am asking you to cooperate with me as you are an important part of my team. I just want you to back out of controlling my life. I will take control now.

"I am asking you to release your control now. I am asking My Higher Self, file and program managers to *uninstall the Inner Conscious Mind's personality selves' operating system* and remove the interface that is operating artificial intelligence and autopilot now. Put them in the trash bin. Delete, erase and destroy all the recreator, reactivator, regenerator, reconstructor and reinstaller virus programs in the back-up files that can reconstruct and reinstall the format that controls and operates autopilot and Inner Conscious Mind's personality selves now. Put them in the trash bin. Delete, erase and destroy all of the programs, patterns, records, operating programs, instructions that Inner Conscious Mind's personality selves function with. I am loving and forgiving you since you did the best you could without my help in the past. I do not want to lose or fight for control again. This will not happen again. I am loving and forgiving you as I know you did the best you could with the programs you had available. I am loving myself and forgiving myself for abdicating my responsibility for myself now. I am 100% committed to taking my power back and taking total control of my life now. I know I can accomplish anything I choose to do now. I am loving and forgiving myself now. I am doing that now. Thank you for your help."

This will give you 100% control over your mind.

Step 11: Remove Inner Conscious Mind's Operating System

Inner Conscious Mind is the one of the three operating systems in Middle Self. It was installed by Conscious Controlling Mind, when we separated from self during a traumatic even in childhood.

It had value as the operating system for auto pilot and artificial intelligence but, after we take control of our life and reclaim our personal power, there is no use for Inner Conscious Mind. If it continues to function in Middle Self, it will try to take control back when we stumble or have to deal with a traumatic situation. It does not like to have any unfinished questions, sentences or actions that cause conflicts in our mind. It will attempt to deal with the conflict causing us to shut down or go into flight or fight to settle the conflict. Most of the time, it will take action in a way we would not approve of if we had control. If we take control, one of the "Catch-22" situations that we can be faced with is that we have 30 seconds to deal with a conflict.

If we lapse and do not take control, Inner Conscious Mind will be reactivated even if we have uninstalled the operating system and it is shut down. It is like an emergency back-up system. If we are confronted with a traumatic situation or a conflict we cannot handle, it will handle it for us. If we are thrown back into survival from a feeling, conflict or situation, it will keep us in balance the best way it can. Its main intents are protection, security and safety. If it feels that we cannot deal with an incident, it put us in denial or an illusion to protect us from an emotional meltdown.

Our main direction in this process is to strengthen clients' ability to empower themselves to handle all conflicts effectively so that Inner Conscious Mind does not have to intervene in any way. When we have reclaimed our personal power to the point that other people's behavior has no effect on us, we will be able to validate ourselves, knowing we are all right under all circumstances. We will not feel threatened in any way, nor will we feel our self-esteem, self-worth and self-confidence are attacked in any way. We will always be able to respond in an effective way in every situation.

Removing Inner Conscious Mind's ability to reactivate will not protect us from going into survival, but it will shift more of the responsibility to ourselves. It will force Conscious Mind to take control because it no longer has a safety net to do its work.

Affirmation to uninstall Inner Conscious Mind's operating system:

"I am asking you Higher Self, File and Program Manager to Uninstall and delete Inner Conscious Mind's operating system, plus all the operating instructions, programs, patterns and records. I am committed to reintegrate Conscious Mind and I am doing this now.

"Remove, delete, erase all operating files, file directories and any programs or beliefs operating in Inner Conscious Mind's operating system. Send them to the trash bin now. Capture, quarantine and remove <u>an infinity number</u> of virus regenerator, recreator, reactivator, reduplicator or reinstaller programs which could reinstall Inner Conscious Mind or any files operating in Inner Conscious Mind at the current time. Send them to the trash bin. Delete all files, and put them in the recylce bin."

Step 12. Reclaiming Personal Power and Getting Conscious Mind to Cooperate with Taking Control Back

During childhood most people at some point we encounter traumatic or fearful experiences which cause them to escape from the fear.

If people have been on autopilot for most of their life or have been in survival for a long period of time, we have found that Conscious mind Splits into three operating systems. It will put up resistance to allowing us to take control back, since it had to step in when we escaped into Magical Child to avoid fear or abuse. When we are hiding in Inner Child, Middle Self moves from being a program manager to being a program creator. True Spiritual Self is pushed into the background since we separated from it, abandoning both it and our control over our mind. What we wanted was an illusion of safety and security. To obtain it we escaped into hiding, which can be considered mental illness.

If we stay in limbo for an extended period of time, our mind sets up a new separate operating system and assigns a name to it. This split or multiple personality becomes who we identify with when we come out of hiding. There is no interface between the original true self and this created false self; they are totally separate operating systems with different programs and files. If this situation happens many times over a period of years, multiple personality selves can be created. Depending on the external conditions, a person can slip from one to the other to escape uncomfortable conflicting situations. These can all be cleared as we did earlier in Step Three.

When a personality self, pattern or habit is cleared, we must check to see if Conscious Mind is in accordance with the work. Check with NK (muscle testing) to make sure we are getting a "yes" as to whether it will work with us. If we receive a "no," we must find out what the resistance is, or we can have a discussion in affirmation form to demand that Conscious Mind work with us. Talking to ourselves to regain control may seem odd, but we must understand who we are. We are attempting to get Conscious Rational decision making Mind to recover its lost self and let us take back control. Under the normal operating system, Conscious Rational Mind accesses the data base using the current programs or writes new programs then passes them to Conscious Mind which sends and receives data to and from Subconscious Mind's database through File Manager (Ego).

Middle Self helps us create programs, which Ego (file Manager) files in the Subconscious Mind. Even when we clear all the operating files, we must still make sure that all the various recreator viruses are cleared as they have their own operating systems that are totally independent of the Conscious Mind's operating system. They can recreate and reinstall old files if we do not take control and reclaim our power over Conscious Mind. It is not as if we are fighting it for control, even though it may seem that way when we try to regain control. Conscious Mind can only operate based on the operating system it has installed and the files and programs it has access to. When we erase and delete that operating system and all the files, we can install a new clear operating system which will allow it to work with us. The Catch-22 again is that we can return to our old habit patterns or we will reactivate all the negative programs that we deleted. Even though we may have cleared all the programs, our Conscious Controlling Mind remembers the past and can reprogram either negatively from the past or positively with new habit patterns—it is our choice. It's all about awareness, desire, intention, determination, commitment, discipline and the willingness to follow through and keep on task, much like walking down the street where someone has left a manhole cover off. You must notice there is no manhole cover there, or you will fall into it.

When we set a goal to change, we must follow through. If we back off from our commitment, procrastinate or fall back into survival, our Conscious Controlling Mind will take over again using the same files and programs from the past. If we continue this pattern, it becomes increasingly more difficult to convince our inner selves that we will meet our commitments and follow through. If we do not discipline ourselves to stay on task, we will have to continually fight for control. Each time we make an attempt to take back control, we must fight harder when we should not have to fight at all.

What this really means is that we cannot focus on the past or any trauma or conflicts from the past. If we continue to tell stories or even repeat the incidents, we will give our mind the message that we have not let them go and it will refocus on them, reinstalling the files over and over until we let the past go.

This is a long affirmation, intended to realign the set up and the function of our mind. The following three parts will reclaim our personal power and give us 100% control over our mind and body. To retain this control, we must pay close attention to what we are reading. We are telling our self and our mind what we are going to do. We must follow through and discipline ourselves to do exactly what we are committing to do in this affirmation. By verbally repeating the following affirmation out loud, we can realign the protocol so that Conscious Mind will be able to function in its proper place, correctly aligned with the protocol within our mind's computer:

We are the programmer, so we can bring the same programs back by thinking or repeating old behavior about fear, lack of control, or feeling inadequate. Conscious Mind's programs will be reinstalled with the same files. We must let go of past behavior, attitudes, perceptions and interpretations of how our life was and accept what is. The intention of this affirmation is to clear all the clutter, garbage, negative programs, patterns and beliefs plus all the operating systems and all the operating instructions that we have collected over the years in the various file systems in Conscious mind.

Affirmation to clear Conscious Mind's operating files:

"In accordance with universal law of free choice and right action, I am asking Conscious Mind to work with me now. I know in my childhood, I withdrew and separated from myself. I lost control of my life. I escaped into Magical Child, and Inner Child took over my life. I gave my power away and let you set up Inner Conscious Mind with autopilot to run my life. I realize you did the best you could with the programs you had available to you at the time. I know when you set up Inner Conscious mind to guide my life with artificial intelligence, you shifted over to Conscious Controlling Mind. This separated my Conscious Mind into three separate operating systems.

"I am committed to reclaiming my personal power now and reintegrating my Conscious Mind and returning to becoming the computer programmer and director of my life now. I realize you accepted that Inner Conscious Mind had control and that you followed along with the decisions that my Personality Selves made for me.

"I am loving myself and forgiving myself for allowing this resistance to build up. I realize now I was not aware of how my Conscious Mind became contaminated with programs that were focused on scarcity, lack, fear, rejection and limitation that were set up to sabotage my personal growth and success in life

"I am asking you, Conscious Mind, to work with me. I am asking you to release your control of Conscious Mind back to me. I have no need to suffer, struggle or to be punished for my past experiences. I accept that I have made mistakes and through time, you have accepted these concepts and programs: *I am not all right, I am not acceptable, I don't fit in, I am unworthy* and self rejection as a functional part of the operating system in my mind. I am demanding you release them all now and let them go permanently. They are creating double binds in my mind and pain in my body.

"I am asking my Higher Self, File and Program Managers to remove the operating system and operating instructions that Conscious Mind has been operating from. Capture, quarantine and remove an <u>infinity number</u> of file folders, file directories, programs, patterns, records, beliefs, concepts, attitudes and interpretations that contain all the operating programs from all file directories that Conscious Mind operates from. Delete, erase and destroy all files and file-folders. Put them in the trash bin, delete them, send them to the recycle bin now. I thank you for your help.

"I am asking Higher Self, File and Program Manager to perform a file scan and a file search for recreator, regenerator, reactivator, reconstructor, replicator, dup-licator, compiler and reinstaller virus programs in my Conscious Mind's and Subconscious Mind's operating systems. Uninstall all operating systems and operating instructions. Capture, quarantine and remove an <u>infinity number</u> of these files, file directories, programs, patterns, records, beliefs, concepts, attitudes, perceptions and interpretations that these programs operate from. Put them in the trash bin, delete, erase and destroy all files and file-folders and put them in the recycle bin. I thank you for your help.

"I am asking you to capture quarantine, delete, erase and destroy and remove an <u>infinity number</u> of programs, patterns, records, beliefs, concepts, attitudes, inter-pretations and perceptions that drive the operating systems for Archive files, Backup files, past, current, present and future Time-Line files, Denial and Denial-of-Denial operating files in my Subconscious Mind. Capture, quarantine and remove, delete, erase and destroy an <u>infinity number</u> of programs, patterns, records, beliefs, concepts, attitudes, interpretations, perceptions and the operating instructions in Conscious and Subconscious Mind's operating files that install and operate these programs, Put them all in the trash bin,, and send them to the recycle bin so they will never affect me again. Thank you for your help.

"I am asking you to do another file scan and a file search for recreator, regenerator, reactivator, reconstructor, replicator, duplicator, compiler and reinstaller virus programs in my Conscious and Subconscious Minds' operating systems that have reinstalled Archive files, Backup files, past, present, current and future Time-Line files, Denial and Denial-of-Denial files in Conscious and Subconscious Minds' operating files. Uninstall all operating systems and operating instructions. Capture, quarantine and remove an <u>infinity number</u> of these files, file directories, programs, patterns, records, beliefs, concepts, attitudes, perceptions and interpretations that these programs operate from. Put them in the trash bin. Delete, erase and destroy all files and the file folders, put them in the recycle bin. I thank you for your help.

"I am asking you to work with me to release all of these programs. Capture, quarantine and remove an <u>infinity number</u> of the operating instructions and operating systems that drive these self-defeating programs, patterns, concepts, attitudes, feelings, perceptions, and interpretations that have created this fear, lack, limitation, scarcity, resistance and pain. Send them to the trash bin. Delete, erase, and destroy them. Send them to recycle bin. I thank you for your help.

"I have the right to live in peace, happiness, harmony, joy and unconditional love and acceptance. I am not skeptical or have any doubts that I can release the pain and heal my body now. I know in the past I had doubts about my abilities and what I could accomplish in my life, I will overcome them and become a success in my life. I am letting go of the past now. I am loving and forgiving all the people who participated in my life and caused me to create the feelings of rejection: *I am not all right, I don't fit in, I am not accepted, I do not have any value,* and feelings of abandonment. I am perfectly all right now. I may have not known that in the past, but I do now. I am helping and supporting others in their efforts to become successful and I know that what you give, you receive back 10-fold and more, as long as you do this without any need for validation and acceptance.

"I am asking you to work with me now. There is no need for resistance, which the pain that you have created in the past has indicated. I have no need to suffer any longer. I demand you work with me and release this pain now. Thank you for your help. I am loving and forgiving myself now.

"I am asking Higher Self, Conscious and Subconscious Mind, Middle Self, File and Program Managers to work with me now to release the dysfunctional programs from [insert program or belief to release] _____ now. I know I am entitled to live in peace, happiness, harmony, joy, unconditional love and acceptance. I know that I am entitled to these qualities, and I have them now.

"I am entitled to be pain-free and agile to do what I chose, as I am working for the betterment of mankind and my fellow beings on this planet. I ask that we all work as a team to create health, wellness and a total state of unconditional love, acceptance and abundance within ourselves. I know we can do this now. I thank you for your help. I am loving and forgiving myself now for allowing this resistance to build up. My Conscious Rational Mind is true self, it is my identity with the spiritual being in me, and I will make the decisions now. It is your responsibility, Conscious Mind, to work with me now. I will make the decisions, programs and direct the actions in my life now. I know we can work together as an effective team now. I will direct all my decisions to you and Middle Self, to be filed by my File Manager in my Subconscious Mind's database. I am loving myself and forgiving myself for having given my power away now. I am taking back my personal power and control now. I am True Self. I am doing that now. Thank you for your help.

"I am asking my Higher Self, File and Program Managers to reinstall a new, clean, functional operating system, free and clear of impostors and saboteurs that could contaminate my mind with fear of failure, limitation, scarcity and lack programs. Install these new operating instructions that support my health, happiness and well-being. Install them in Conscious Mind now. Wellness is a total state of being, and I am entitled to this state of mind now. Thank you for your help."

Step 13 Taking Control of Conscious Controlling Mind

In steps 11 and 12, we were assuming that Conscious Rational Mind (CRM) would back down and allow us to take control, step in and become the programmer and director of our mind. In many situations this is not the case.

We have discovered that CRM is the controller in our mind and has the qualities and behavior patterns we describe as EGO behavior. If you are not in control of your mind's actions, then CRM has taken control in childhood. Very few people have taken control back from it. The reason I describe it as *rational* is that it *thinks* it is rational in its basic behavior. CRM's main role in your life is protection, safety and security. It will do whatever it must do to provide this service to you. Many times, CRM's behavior is irrational and operates from an illusion it feels is the right action to take. This explains why people become self-righteous, controlling, resistant or argumentative. If we were in control of our mind, we would not *react* but would *respond* in an effective manner. Conversely, CRM operates and controls from fear. It puts limitations on us and doesn't allow us to explore what could be beneficial to us if it feels that it threatens its control. I have actually found people would rather suffer in pain or a disability, and avoid finding out what is causing the breakdown or disability. Many people will avoid or claim they are all right the way they are, when you can clearly observe they are not. It may be a battle to tale over control if CRM senses you are not willing to confront everything with commitment and discipline.

When we confront our limitations and take control, CRM will give you control, but if you drop the ball, CRM is back in control and will throw you right back into survival. At first, it does not take much to throw you off balance. A simple feeling of: "I am not accepted," or, "I am rejected" will cause you to fall back. This why we focus in on self-value and self-validation and acknowledgement. You must do it yourself. You cannot look outside of yourself for validation. If you do, CRM will not let go of control or will take back control. It can be simple or an ongoing battle. Business or financial success will not correlate with personal development if you will yourself through life. We wonder why successful people die when they have it all together. So it seems on the surface but inside, they are in turmoil and do not even know it. They are living a life of illusion. When the responsibility bell tolls, they have to recognize their failure to go for personal development the same way they pushed themselves through business and financial success. Quite often, a person may be the most generous, supportive helping person, yet destroy him or herself from the inside out. Personal health is not just eating right. It's what's eating you from the *inside* that destroys you. CRM can be our major supporter, and we can use it for success at all levels, just as it can be our destroyer. We also discovered CRM was the operating system that controlled our beliefs. If it does not go along with a path you may want to explore, it will block you and create a resistance to that path until you decide to unblock and erase the belief. Some times, it takes a demonstration of a situation over a period of time for CRM to accept that a behavior or process is right for you. When we become CRM, then real success can happen.

Until we recognized the power of Conscious Controlling Mind, we assumed that we could take control by using affirmations to erase and delete programs and operating systems. With all the other affirmations, this was true. We found that we could delete and erase the malfunctioning operating system and/or program, install a new operating system and program, and bingo, we had changed the behavior or healed the illness or disease. In most cases, this will work effectively unless clients have deeply imprinted and imbedded programs, or they do not want to take responsibility for their condition and situation. Our mind may allow us to change many programs as long as it does not challenge or confront Conscious Controlling Mind's control. With Conscious Controlling Mind, we have a very different situation, as it is an interactive operating system that is also the programmer for our mind. It can make decisions and write program software. It will function and set up programs on its own, without our help or input as it has done up until we take control and reclaim our personal power. However, what I thought was a simple task of setting out the path and accomplishing the goal of taking over control was not as easy as I thought. I did not understand how much power Conscious Rational Mind (CRM) could wield, or how powerful it was. I had agreed with the general assumption that Subconscious was the powerhouse because it had over 80% control. But I discovered (as I have said before) it has no power. It is just a database that stores information and software programs. Now that we have discovered the real power in our mind it can be the culprit that blocks and puts limitations on us or it can be a very power force in our success as it has over 90% of the control over our mind in our life. All other segments of our mind basically are controlled by Conscious Controlling Mind.

After using step 12 and 13 for six months, I recognized I was going to have to modify them and add a step 14 to reinstall Conscious Rational Mind (True Self). I noticed in my own case that many times I was being sabotaged by my own mind. Many other clients were reporting the same situation. We found that the deeper the programs were locked in, the more complex it was to remove them. We discovered that, with most people, we can release programs with little resistance. But with some cases, strong family core cultural values will block releases. As a result, CRM will hold onto these core values. We have to do a separate affirmation to clear and release family core values so we can change core value systems.

I discovered that when we eliminated all the programs, patterns, operating systems, and sub-personalities that Conscious Mind was operating from, we had also deleted the safety net that Conscious Rational Mind used to control our behavior. It will cling onto control if we leave any programs in its operating system that it can use. It is all about self-responsibility. We must develop determination with a burning desire to commit to change. It takes discipline to follow through. If you have any doubts about your direction or your ability to make the commitment to take control of your life, CRM will assume it has taken care of you up until now and will fight for control. If you can demonstrate willingness for self-responsibility by taking action, CRM will let you have control.

The Special Relationships with Self.

Most people have special relationships with themselves that support their basic behavior patterns with illusions. We are inside the illusion so we cannot recognize it and will defend and justify our behavior assuming nothing is wrong. Most observers can recognize this behavior is off course and causes resistance. These will be attitudes and/or habit patterns that are blocked from our awareness because they support our personality self. They are what we use to get validation, acceptance and recognition. The main conflict is that they do not get us the respect and recognition we desire, because they alienate people by being seen as self-righteous, manipulating and controlling. Many people call them "ego qualities" but we have seen earlier that Ego has no agenda. These qualities are characterized by controlling conversations, over-talking people in discussion before others finish speaking, or redirecting the conversation to another person or subject. Some people describe this as "hijacking the conversation." Our mind's payoff in doing this is: "If people allow me to take over, control or redirect the conversation, I am being accepted and validated." Our mind is irrational in its viewpoint so it will do whatever it feels will get attention in any form. If we are in control, we know that this behavior will only get us rejection and loss of respect. This is an external reaction to a special relationship

An internal reaction to special relationships is directed to self- rejection, as in: "People do not accept me, I do not fit in, I do not have value so I do not have respect from others, they do not recognize me, I feel inadequate, I'm afraid of groups, I see people as judging me." We even create interpretations about what people think about us when, in fact, they do not even know who we are.

This behavior reaction creates an incongruent message that is projected out from our inner self, so that people pick up a perception of who we are without us even speaking a word. Many people wonder why they are not accepted or excluded from groups and never know why.

The special relationship is illusive, as it covers itself up very well with illusions so we will not catch on to it, even though the casual observer can spot it immediately. It is self-defeating, because as we set ourselves up as the authority on the controlling side and do not recognize we are causing people to reject us from groups, jobs, and positions, since they view such individuals as uncooperative based on the incongruent message they are transmitting. On the outward fear side we escape feeling we are not accepted and rejected.

To release the special relationship, you must find what it is, and then tailor the affirmation to clear the specific formats, beliefs and interpretations held in Conscious Controlling Mind. All special relationships are held in this operating system as it is the one that directs your life (if it is connected up, that is).

The Written 21-day affirmation:

If we have conflicts with beliefs, attitudes, habits or programs that seem to continue block your ability to take control let go of sub personality program that cause conflicts this affirmation will drive the concept in and release them.

This is the ultimate "take responsibility" affirmation. Quite often, to convince ourselves and to get our mind to cooperate, we must take control and lock this in. If we have any challenges that are resistant and keeping reoccuring and reacting on us we can use this affirmation in taking control and responsibility over any aspect or situation in our life we must write the 21-day affirmation to reclaim personal power and take responsibility. This affirmation for the 21-day program must be handwritten 21 times a day for 21 days. In this manner we are sending the information to our mind kinesthetically by writing, visually by reading as we write and verbally by repeating it ourselves as we write too. This drives it in and eventually rewrites the program. I have seen major changes if it is done in the proper manner with commitment and discipline. It must be written 21 times each day. If you miss the full 21 times between the time you wake up and go to sleep, start over from day one again until you succeed in finish the 21 days.

Instructions for use of the 21-day Affirmation:

Insert belief, attitude and/or program that you can not let go or release in 1st line do not enter more than three items. Enter item to release in 2nd line.

Written 21-day affirmation:

"I am 100% committed to taking responsibility for my life now. I recognize that I gave my power away to these negative beliefs. [insert situation to release] _____ I am loving myself and forgiving myself for giving my power away. I know I can take my power back now. I releasing myself from [insert situation to affirm] _____. I am reclaiming my personal power and I am doing that now. I am doing that now, and I am reclaiming it now. I am doing that now. I am 100% committed to following through with this program now."

The written 21-day affirmation allows Inner Conscious Mind to operate in concert with the two other operating systems in the Conscious Mind. We are integrating all three levels of the Conscious Mind so eventually they join up and work as one, as they were intended to. At birth, they are all one operating system, but they get splintered and separated into three operating systems as a survival program. This becomes the personality selves operating the mind. Many therapists feel they must do what they call "soul recovery" and/or call back the spirit to rebuild the splintered separated selves. It is the Conscious Mind that was split and separated; the Soul and spirit are intact with no loss of ability. They are watching us and wondering when we are going to take our power back and learn how to ask and listen to them. We must reclaim our power and eliminate personality selves.

The following affirmation is set up to remove all the operating systems and programs that are malfunctioning and install a clear new system that will work with us. It will break down the resistance so you can take control and become self-validating, placing value on yourself.

Affirmation to Take Control of Conscious Controlling Mind

"In accordance with free will and the law of right action, I am claiming my right to reclaim my personal power now. I recognize, Conscious Controlling Mind, that you have resistance to letting go of control and working with me. I realize now, that I gave you power and control over my mind without realizing I did so. When I was a child I couldn't handle the situations with personal power and take control of my life. I am releasing myself from the fear, anger and all the blame I placed on myself to invalidate myself for not being able to function effectively in my life. I realize I bought into all the attitudes and behavior patterns, that my parents put on me and I didn't realize that they were programming me for the rest of my life. My parents did the best they could under the circumstances, and with the knowledge and resources they had available to them. I am loving and forgiving them now.

"I am committed to taking responsibility for my life now because I realize now it is my responsibility to take control of my life now. I know full well that I held a lot of blame and anger and resentment against myself. I recognize that I invalidate myself for not being able to succeed as I chose to do. I didn't recognize that I was my own worst enemy and I know now that you used that against me to hold to control of my mind. I realize now, it is my responsibility to take control back and to take responsibility for every action in my life. I refuse to allow you to sabotage and control my life any longer. I demand that you release control now. I am not going to fight with you for control any longer.

"I am letting go of all my limitations, and I know I can claim my freedom, by knowing that all I need to do is accept it now. I am doing this now. I realize in the past that I allowed you take control, not knowing what I had done. You want to hold on to that control, because you think that you have better knowledge to take care of me than I can. I know who I am and what my desires and intentions are and I am going to follow my path to success – I will to take control now. I know I can handle any situation or circumstances now and in the future with personal power, ease and acceptance. I realize now, it is my responsibility to take control completely and I realize now I _will_ take control now – you have no choice – I demand you give me control now. I am not going to fight with you over control any longer.

"Since you have not been willing to cooperate with me I am asking you Higher Self, file and program manager to uninstall all operating systems, all operating instructions, all patterns, programs and records that drive Conscious Rational Mind's operating systems. Capture, quarantine and remove and infinity number of these files, file directories, patterns, programs and records, beliefs, concepts and attitudes, perceptions and interpretations that conscious rational mind operated from. Take these programs, patterns and records out of all files. Make sure that they are removed from all directories, all sub-directories, and all operating systems and put them in the trash bin. Delete and erase all files, all file folders, and make sure they are sent to the Recycle Bin now.

"I am asking Higher Self, file and program managers to do a file scan and a file search to make sure that all invalidator, self rejection and self-defeating programs, patterns and records, attitudes, perceptions and interpretations that created fear, lack and limitation, scarcity and resistance are removed from conscious rational mind now. And put them in the Recycle Bin.

"I am also asking you to capture, quarantine, delete, erase and destroy an infinity number of all programs, patterns and records, beliefs and concepts, attitudes and interpretations and perceptions that drive the operating systems for archive files, backup files, past, current, present and future time line files, denial and denial of denial operating files which are functioning in conscious rational mind. Put them all in the trash bin, lock them up and seal them up and put them in the Recycle Bin.

"Do a file scan and file search for all recreator, regenerator, reactivator, reconstructor, replicator, duplicator, compiler, and reinstaller virus programs that recreate programs in my Conscious Rational Mind. Delete, erase and destroy all of these virus program recreaters, along with all their operating systems, operating programs and instructions, and put them in the trash bin, lock them up and put them in the Recycle Bin. I know you are doing that now. I thank you for your help.

"Each person that came into my life had a lesson to teach me, and many times I was asking for their validation to gain my value. Quite often they programmed me without me even understanding what they were doing. I know I can release them now. I am forgiving loving and accepting them, knowing they did the best they could. I realize now, it is my responsibility to take control of my life now. I am committed to doing that now. I am determined to succeed in my life now. And I am not accepting your control any longer. I know that I have the right to take responsibility, and I refuse to live in pain and suffering and struggle any longer. I refuse to punish myself and procrastinate any longer. I know I am all right. I do have value and other people will acknowledge me when I start validating and acknowledging myself. I am doing that now. I am a self-validated person. I know I have dynamic value other people will recognize my value now as I am placing value on myself. I do not need others to validate me any longer. I am loving myself and forgiving myself, I am doing that now

"I know I have the right to live in peace, happiness, harmony and joy, unconditional love and acceptance, and that is my choice. I am asking you Higher Self, file and program manager to install a new operating system with a new set of operating programs that operates and functions effectively, and that allows me to live functionally in peace, happiness, harmony and joy, unconditional love, unconditional acceptance, allowing me to have full control over my conscious rational mind now. I am the Conscious Rational Mind.

"I am the computer programmer and I will run Conscious Rational Mind from now on. I realize that Conscious Rational Mind is my true self and I can identify with true self now. Because I do have the power, I do have the control, and I know now that I will work to succeed and function at the highest level of my consciousness. And I know now, that I will integrate with conscious mind, subconscious mind, middle self and ego – we will all work together as a team to create success, abundance and knowing well that I do have intrinsic value. I have full control over my life now, and I refuse to give up control again because I am in control now.

"I accept the fact that I have the ability to succeed now. I accept that now. Wellness is a total state of Being, and I am entitled to this state of mind now, I accept it now, knowing full well I can function within myself at the highest level of my consciousness because I am self-validating now. I thank you for your help, I am loving myself and forgiving myself for having run away from myself, Giving my power away and allowed my Conscious Controlling Mind to control me. I am loving myself and forgiving myself and releasing myself from control. I am taking my power back now. I am doing that now. I am loving and forgiving myself for creating separation within myself. I am integrating Conscious Mind now.

Note: If you get thrown back into survival from a conflict or confrontation. Go to step 14 read the affirmation it will reestablish balance again.

After reading this affirmation check File and Program Manager. If the are checking positive then you have realigned the operating systems, If they check negative read step 12 again this will rebalance the mind.

Step 14: Reclaiming Personal Power; Returning Control Back to True Self; Getting Conscious Controlling Mind to Reintegrate

Note: If you get thrown back into survival from a conflict or confrontation. This affirmation will reestablish balance again.   After reading this affirmation check File and Program Manager. If the are checking positive then you have realigned the operating systems.

Once we get Conscious Mind to cooperate with us with us, then we must reinstall True Spiritual Self back into the Middle Self operating system. This may be what some teachers describe as soul or spirit recovery. The odd part about this is that soul, spirit, and higher self have been watching the game we have been playing with our life, wondering when we are going to step in and take control. They know exactly what's happening and how to handle it … if we could only take notice and listen to their guidance. The challenge is, how do we listen to their message?

The challenge is to get all of Conscious Mind reintegrated as one unit. The controlling aspect of our mind has taken over and acts out in the form we describe as Ego because it is trying to protect us and keep us safe and secure. It operates from flight or fight. The further we distance ourselves from our original operating system, the harder it is to hear the message. As children, we do not understand this concept, so all we are looking for is safety, security, acceptance and love. When we cannot obtain it from our parents, we look for an escape hatch. We may not know it but, no matter what we have accomplished or how successful we are, we may be playing by the concepts and beliefs about how to be successful and not understanding the universal law of abundance. If so, then we are confronting and fighting with ourselves to maintain our success. If that is true, then we are subject to illness, disease, emotional breakdown and possible total meltdown, both physically and emotionally, if we keep trying to push against the flow. When all the protocols in our life are aligned, then we find it is much easier to accomplish our goals. It is not a continual battle any longer. Now that we have Conscious Controlling Mind willing to give up control and reintegrate and make Conscious Mind whole again we can begin our journey to enlightenment and transformation.

This affirmation realigns us with True Spiritual Self. Everything flows easily downhill. Illness and disease become things of the past, as we no longer need them to teach us a lesson. Support and help become a normal way of working with others. We no longer need validation, as we can accept ourselves as all right. There is one Catch-22 in this, though—when you move into total balance in your self, you may appear as a tornado to unclear people who cannot walk into the peace in your center. They may be afraid, resentful or fearful of who you are; the external winds of your invisible tornado may throw them. Their illusion will cause them to see you as self-righteous and arrogant rather than self-validating, self-confident with high self-esteem, and self-worth

This affirmation will get all the operating systems in your mind into alignment, so we function as the computer programmer and director/CEO of your life. True Spiritual Self will be installed and we have healed the separation from self and become whole again.

Affirmation to Reclaim Personal Power:

"In accordance with universal law of free choice and right action, now that I have reclaimed my personal power, I realize I pushed aside True Self and separated from myself, losing control when I was a child. I was not aware of how to control my life and escaped into Magical Child survival mode to avoid the fear I was feeling. I recognize now that I ran away from myself and escaped into Inner Child to get away from the fear because I could not control my feelings and emotions. I am forgiving myself for running away from self.

"I am committed to reintegrating my Conscious Mind into one unit now. I recognize it is my responsibility to love and forgive myself, knowing that nobody did anything to me. I did not know this when I was child. I can release myself from the fear now and let go of blame and resentment. Each person who came into my life had a lesson to teach me, yet I was unaware of, nor could I understand, their message at the time. I am forgiving, accepting all the people who passed through my life with lessons I did not recognize at the time. I am releasing any blame, anger or resentment I may have held against them. They were unable to provide me the love and validation I wanted because they did not know what love was themselves. I am loving and forgiving them now.

"I am grateful that I can see now that I was living in fear, lack, scarcity, resentment and invalidating myself with the belief that others were blocking my success and not validating me. I know I have to validate myself. Other people cannot do it for me. I must do it myself. I am validating myself now. I know now that the universe is abundant and that we all can have what we desire when we recognize we are the only one who can put limitations on ourselves and block our abundance. I am accepting the abundance of the universe and my ability to accept my success. I have it now!

"I just did not recognize that it was right in front of me. I am entitled to live in peace, happiness, harmony, joy, unconditional love and abundance. I know I have it now. I know I can accept every situation as it is, without judgment or justification. I accept nonresistance as my path in life I must follow. I accept everything as it is without resistance knowing that what is, is. I accept my path in life without any need to change, control, manipulate any person or circumstances. Resistance causes pain, suffering and struggle. I know I can view everything and every situation as a lesson in acceptance, which will release me from pain, suffering and struggle. I know I must recognize and validate myself, knowing I am all right, before others will acknowledge me. I am letting go of all my limitations. I am validating myself. I doing this now. I know that I can claim my freedom by knowing that all I need to do is accept it. I am doing this now.

"I know I can live in the present, accepting what is now. I have and can move through every lesson, accepting that I will accomplish anything I choose to do because I am free of limitation, lack and scarcity. Abundance of love, acceptance, validation, and success are my responsibility. I accept this now. I am loving and forgiving myself now. Everything I choose manifests for me now. I am choosing success at all levels of my life—physically, mentally, emotionally and spiritually now.

"I am committed to following the path Higher Power has provided for me. I will listen to the guidance and messages that my True Self provides for me. I know I can handle any situation or circumstance now and in the future with personal power, ease and acceptance. True Self is my source of guidance. I will confront every challenge directly and never escape, abandon or run away from self again. I am loving myself and forgiving myself for avoiding and escaping from responsibility in the past. I will confront, control and handle every issue and feeling before it becomes an emotion, making a positive resolution with every issue. I am Conscious Rational Mind and I am reinstalling True Spiritual Self back in my mind now. I have healed the separation from self. I loving and forgiving myself knowing that I am complete and whole now. I accept this now."

Step 15: Release, delete and erase sub-personalities

Sub-personalities can be used to track a person's growth and progress as they will indicate where the breakdowns and challenges are in changing habit patterns. They will indicate the weaknesses where clients are having difficulty in dealing with themselves and other people. When you have cleared them all and you are testing a client in the next session, the number that get back in will indicate how much responsibility the client is taking to handle and control in their life.

Go through the list of autopilot and validation sub-personalities and check those on the list. (Tip: photocopy the page and use it each time you do a clearing.) Check for all virus activators in back-up files. These will recreate the program or sub-personality after it has been removed unless they are removed and deleted along with the operating file. Use the first affirmation to remove all of the control sub-personalities as a group so you can work effectively. They will try to interfere if not removed. Then go to the second group, which do not have to be released in the first session. When finished, go to the second affirmation to complete the process.

Basic six sub-personalities:

- Survival Self
- Instinctual Self
- Inner Child
- Critical Parent
- Inner Adult
- Shadow Self

You can take the programs they have created to support themselves and delete them, but they cannot be removed, erased and destroyed as these are indigenous operating systems that were installed in the mind at birth. Quite often, people want to separate Inner Child from themselves, blaming it for their problems. When someone says, "My Inner Child was hurt," they are trying to avoid taking responsibility.

Inner Child is part of the autopilot's operating system and will work with MCS and AI to run your life. It can only record a feeling and/or interpretation as it is part of their mind and is part of who we are. It may have had to take over working through autopilot and artificial intelligence, but it has no control over your life when and if you decide to take responsibility for your behavior. It can only operate through programs that it creates through program manager (Middle Self). When we take our power back and reclaim control over ourselves and remove MCS, inner child grows up and drops out. Some of these sub-personalities can number in the hundreds of thousands to the millions because they build up exponentially from birth. I have found up to 6 million Controllers and 3.9 million Procrastinators. We discovered that we could use ***an infinity number*** rather than count each one. In this way, we can release them much more quickly without getting into the details of the exact number.

Few therapy processes access sub-personalities in any workable way. Practitioners will access them or bring them up but seldom do they get released so you may find a buildup in the millions. I have worked with clients who say they have been working on themselves for years, thinking they were accomplishing progress yet had moved very little in their journey. We find that the therapists with whom they worked were having more problems because the therapists they had seen were bringing programs to the surface, assuming that by becoming aware of them, they were releasing them. Many times, you will find that releasing the sub-personalities will make a major change in a person's life. After releasing the sub-personalities, you must go to the file programs that the sub-personalities created and clear them out, too.

A Group 1 sub-personality is the committee chairman that controls the committee of sub-personalities. Most therapies will bring them up but do not release the programs they operate through. They will be present in large numbers as they accumulate from birth. If a client has done considerable work in trying to get clear, you could find millions of sub-personalities, but we no longer need to count them.

All these sub-personalities operate through Conscious Mind and are created by Middle Self. They are created when we do not deal well with a given situation. When they are used over and over, they become the personality selves blocking out our true self.

The following should be done in the first or second session. If there is not enough time in the first session, delay it until the second.

Using NK to check for each sub-personality or program, go through each group and put a check mark next to each one that is operating on the pages. Once you have compiled all the sub-personalities and programs, go through each group, stating, "I am putting them in the trash bin."

"In accordance with universal law and free choice, I am asking file and program manager to go through all the veils, shields, illusions, and delusions, and bring up all programs, patterns, records, programs and sub-personalities, so we can access them now."

Group 1: Autopilot sub-personalities:

"I am asking file and program manager to remove *an infinity number* of:
- ___ External Controller Sub-personality from Subconscious Mind
- ___ Internal Controller Sub-personality from Subconscious Mind
- ___ Internal Controller Sub-personality from the denial files, denial-of-denial
- ___ Justifier (the mind justifying its reactions)
- ___ Rationalizer (you justifying your reactions)
and put them in the trash bin."

Group 2: Controller sub-personalities:

"I am asking file and program managers to remove _an infinity number_ of:

- _____ **Power Controller Sub-personalities from Subconscious Mind (controls others)**
- _____ **Authority Figure (needs to be right)**
- _____ **Controller (has to be in control of all activities)**
- _____ **Self Righteous (I have all the answers)**
- _____ **Know it all (has to be the authority on the situation/incident)**
- _____ **Manipulator (must have it his/her way)**
- _____ **Competitor (Has to be first and the best)**
- _____ **Interrogator (always checking people out)**
- _____ **Arrogance (I am better than or I know it all)**
- _____ **Intimidator (tries to control by threat or fear)**
- _____ **Victimizer (takes advantage and manipulates)**
- _____ **Destroyers (delights in causing conflicts)**
- _____ **Rebel (has resistance to any authority)**
- _____ **Aloof (I don't care, but wants attention)**
- _____ **Military Leader (Regimental controller, my way is the only way)**
- _____ **Warrior (many times controlled by Shadow Self, likes to fight)**
- _____ **Ingratitude (I am entitled to it, unwilling to show appreciation)**
- _____ **Annoyer (does not know how to get attention in an appropriate way)**
- _____ **Betrayer (Wants others to do the dirty work.) and put them in the trash bin."**

Group 3: External Validation sub-personalities:

"**I am asking File and Program Manager to remove *an infinity number* of:**
- **___ Empathizer**
- **___ Rescuer**
- **___ Hero**
- **___ Savior**
- **___ Healer**
- **___ Protector**
- **___ Winner**
- **___ Martyr**
- **___ Warrior**
- **___ Mother figure**
- **___ Messiah Complex**
- **___ Father Figure**
- **___ Guru**
- **___ People pleaser**
- **___ War Hero**
and put them in the trash bin."

Group 4: Victim sub-personalities:

"I am asking file and program Manager to remove _an infinity number_ of:

- __ Procrastinator
- __ Avoider
- __ Confuser
- __ Vacillator
- __ Indecisive
- __ Disorientor
- __ Disorganizer
- __ Disassociator
- __ Distractor
- __ Judger
- __ Resenter
- __ Pulling sympathy
- __ Saboteur
- __ Impatience
- __ Sacrificer
- __ Projector
- __ Gullible
- __ Invalidator
- __ Counter dependent
- __ Codependent

- ___ Poor Me/self pity
- ___ Struggler/striver
- ___ Sufferer/victim
- ___ Jealous /selfish
- ___ Pain Addict
- ___ Envious
- ___ Self Pity
- ___ Scardy Cat
- ___ Nagger
- ___ Chameleon
- ___ Substance abuser
- ___ Refusal to take responsibility
- ___ Blamer
- ___ Make my decisions for me
- ___ Masochist
- ___ Vampire
- ___ Liar
- ___ Runaway
- ___ Damsel in Distress
- ___ Soap Opera Star

and put them in the trash bin."

Group 5: Programs and Feelings:

"I am asking file and program managers to remove _an infinity number of_:

- __ **Feeling of futility**
- __ **Frustration**
- __ **Physical Blocker**
- __ **Spiritual Blocker**
- __ **I am not all right**
- __ **I am not acceptable**
- __ **I am unworthy**
- __ **Shadow termination program**
- __ **Lack of self-esteem, self-worth**
- __ **Mental Blocker (Causes Blackouts)**
- __ **Energy Blocker (low Energy)**
- __ **I am not entitled to live**
- __ **I want to stay sick for attention**

- ___ **I don't fit in**
- ___ **I am not accepted**
- ___ **God rejects me**
- ___ **Feeling Sorry For Self**
- ___ **Nobody Cares For Me**
- ___ **Lack of Trust**
- ___ **Lack of Self Respect**

and put them in the trash bin."

Group 6: Rejection and abandonment programs

"**I am asking file and program manager to** remove *an infinity number* **of:**

Rejection programs:
- __ **Rejection by mother**   •___ **People do not trust me**
- __ **Rejection by father**   •___ **People reject me**
- __ **Rejected by others**   •___ **People reject what I say**
- __ **People reject who I am**   •___ **People don't like me**
- __ **Rejection by partner (husband, wife, girl friend, boy friend)**

Anger programs:
- __ **Anger at not being able to get ahead (blaming it on others)**
- __ **Anger at being rejected and/or abandoned**
- __ **Anger at not being respected**
- __ **Anger at not being recognized**
- __ **Anger at having to accept responsibility**
- __ **Anger at not being accepted**
- __ **Refusal to reach out**
- __ **Anger at having to reach out**
- __ **Anger at moving forward**
- __ **Anger at having to step forward**
- __ **Using anger to control**

Fear programs:
- __ **Fear of having to take responsibility**
- __ **Fear of being rejected**   •___ **Fear of reaching out**
- __ **Fear of vulnerability**   •___ **Fear of venturing forward**
- __ **Feeling inadequate**   •___ **Fear of Emasculation**
- __ **Fear of being abandoned**   •___ **Fear of Failure**
- __ **Fear of Success**
      and put them in the trash bin."

When you have placed them all in the trash bin use the following affirmation to delete, erase and destroy them.

Affirmation to delete, erase and destroy trash bin contents:

"In accordance with universal law of free choice, I am asking My Higher Self, File and Program Managers to *uninstall all the operating systems* from all files. *Capture, quarantine and remove all* the sub-personalities, programs and files that have been placed in the trash bin. Remove, delete, erase and destroy all programs, patterns, records, all operating instructions, programs and systems from Conscious Mind, Inner Conscious Mind, Middle Self, Subconscious Mind's operating files, past, present, current, simultaneous and future time-line files, denial, no perception of denial-of-denial, back up, unmarked and mismatched files, mislabeled, unlabeled files, untitled files, orphan files, forgotten files, ghost, neglected and all restricted files that have been prohibited, forbidden, distorted, aborted, damaged and locked away as unavailable or unopenable. *Remove an Infinity number* of recreator, regenerator, reactivator, reconstructor, reinstaller virus programs from the back up files. Lock them all up and put them in the trash bin. Burn and incinerate them now. I thank you for your help. I am loving myself and forgiving myself now."

Note: The following steps are optional. Do not use in the first session if there is not enough time or if there are other issues that have priority or must be handled.

Notice please read before going to the next step

Steps 16 - 20 are no longer required. Steps 13 and 14 clear and delete the programs contained in steps 16 -20. They have been left in to demonstrate the programs that are controlling our mind.
Read them for information. You do not have to perform them.

Step 16: Remove Magical Child Syndrome

Note: Magical Child is the computer's 'safe mode' place where a child finds safety and security.

Magical Child has two sides to it. The positive side is the imaginative state a child can enter to daydream and play with imaginative playmates. We have run into situations where people were having problems with repeating or understanding the affirmations. In the past, I assumed this was resistance created by their mind that was causing the lapse. I have found a few people who were having major problems verbalizing the affirmations. I checked their hearing to see if they could hear me properly and found that this was not the problem as they had 100% hearing. They would leave words out or be unable to comprehend and completely understand the affirmation. They would mispronounce the words throughout the session. In the past, I assumed this was because this process was new and very confrontational and never checked any further. When I checked in more detail, I discovered that, when we accessed the programs, they were reverting to a time in childhood where they had experienced a traumatic situation.

It was becoming more prevalent, so I worked to find the cause. I was aware of Magical Child Syndrome (MCS) from my experience with children who had been through extremely traumatic experiences. Now it was popping up in adults who had been through traumatic experiences as a child. Not only that—we found that it was not necessarily the severity of the experience, but the *perception* of the experience that caused the program to be installed. A victim can make a mountain out of a mole hill, which results in MCS programs to be installed where others who have been in similar experiences let it go with no consequences or MCS programs. So, I reasoned, it is the *interpretation* about how the person feels about the experience, and not necessarily the severity of the experience that causes MCS programs to be installed. Whether the perception of the incident causes MCS to be installed comes down to whether the individual is a survivor or a victim.

As a result, we are now testing everyone for Magical Child Syndrome, and find that more than 70% of clients are functioning from MCS. This will also activate artificial intelligence, so we must remove that operating system. We have found that MCS functions through the Inner Child sub-personality. In some cases, Inner Child does not want to let go of MCS as it has become quite comfortable operating through it. Now I ask Inner Child if it will let go of MCS before we say the affirmation. People who identify with Inner Child from Twelve-step groups may have an attachment to Inner Child, so they separate it from themselves and hold onto it as a separate self. In this case, it can become a split personality self. At this point, it becomes an operating system in the mind. It can take some gentle discussion to get Inner Child to let go of its hold on MCS. We have set up an affirmation to ask Inner Child to release MCS and take responsibility. When it can feel safe and secure, it will release MCS.

All sub-personalities can become operating systems acting through artificial intelligence and autopilot. (To review examples of MCS, see my book *Your Body Is Talking; Are You Listening?*) Ask:

"Is Magical Child Syndrome is operating in the mind?"
"Inner Child, are you willing to release Magical Child Syndrome?"

If the answer is no, use the first affirmation below to request Inner Child's help. If the answer is yes, go to the second affirmation to release MCS.

Affirmation to request Inner Child's help:

"In accordance with universal law of free choice and right action, I am asking my Inner Child to work with me now. I realize that I gave my power away, letting autopilot and artificial intelligence take over to escape from fear and trauma. I am ready and willing to face it now. I am committed to taking responsibility and reclaiming my personal power now. I know I must take control over my life now. Thank you for reconciling with me and cooperating with me, so that I can fulfill my role to you as a loving parent."

(Affirmation to release Magical Child Syndrome on next page)

Affirmation to release Magical Child Syndrome:

"I realize now that when I was a child, I went through a traumatic experience where I was afraid and felt threatened. I escaped that fear by creating and installing Magical Child Syndrome. I know that I can release it now. I am asking my Higher Self, file and program managers to *uninstall the operating systems* and put them in the trash bin. Capture, quarantine and remove *an infinity number* of Magical Child syndrome programs and split personality programs from Conscious Mind, Middle Self, and Subconscious Mind's operating files, denial, no perception of denial-of-denial, past, present, parallel and future time-line files, back-up files and all other files that have been opened. Put them in the trash bin. Remove, delete, erase and destroy all interfaces with shadow selves and artificial intelligence, programs, patterns and records, all operating instructions, operating systems and operating programs that drive magical child syndrome. Remove all recreator, reactivator, regenerator, and reinstaller viruses. Put them in the trash bin. Burn and incinerate them now. Thank you for your help. I am loving and forgiving myself now."

Step 17: Remove Critical Parent

Critical Parent is a program that is an operating program file installed in our mind from birth. It tends to pick up all the negative programming we hear from adults when we are growing up. If we are not validated and supported as child, Critical Parent will mimic all our parents' behavior that was directed at us. All we need to do is remove the operating system and instructions, and it will be erased, deleted, and eliminated from our mind. I do not understand why this file is placed in our mind, but it must be deleted or it will control our behavior throughout our life.

(See next page for Affirmation)

Affirmation for removing Critical Parent:

"I recognize that as a child I gave my power away to automatic pilot. You picked up all the negative input I allowed my mind to accept and record. I refuse to allow you to run my life any longer. I refuse to accept your critical negative reaction to everything I am doing. I will succeed at every project I set up to accomplish.

"I am asking my Higher Self, file and program managers to *uninstall all the operating systems that Critical Parent operates from* and put them in the trash bin. Capture, quarantine and remove *an infinity number* of Critical Parent programs from Conscious Mind, Middle Self, and Subconscious Mind's operating files, denial, no perception of denial-of-denial, past, present, parallel and future time-line files, back-up files and all other files that have been opened.

"Put them in the trash bin. Remove, delete, erase and destroy all interfaces with shadow selves and artificial intelligence, programs, patterns and records, all operating instructions, operating systems and operating programs that drive Magical Child Syndrome. Remove all recreator, reactivator, regenerator, and reinstaller viruses. Put them in the trash bin. Burn and incinerate them now. Thank you for your help. I am loving and forgiving myself now."

Step 18: Removing Inner Critic

Inner Critic is similar to the Critical Parent. It assumes our thoughts, feelings, and self-talk, and feeds them back to us. If we tell ourselves; "I am not accepted," "I reject myself," "I do not fit in," "I am afraid of failure," and all the other negative feelings we tell ourselves, it will set us up to fail. It reinforces lack of self-esteem, inferiority, denial, avoidance, lack of self-confidence, procrastination, disorientation, motivation and all the feelings that cause us not to take action in our life. It sets up the illusions that we operate from.

(See next page for Affirmation)

Affirmation for removing Inner Critic:

"I recognize that as a child I gave my power away to automatic pilot. You picked up all the negative input I allowed my mind to accept and record. I refuse to allow you to run my life any longer. I refuse to accept your critical negative reaction to everything I am doing. I will succeed at every project I set up to accomplish. I am taking control of my life now.

"I am asking my Higher Self, file and program managers to *uninstall all the operating systems that Inner Critic operates from* and put them in the trash bin. Capture, quarantine and remove *an infinity number* of Inner Critic programs from Conscious Mind, Middle Self, and Subconscious Mind's operating files, denial, no perception of denial-of-denial, past, present, parallel and future time-line files, back-up files and all other files that have been opened. Put them in the trash bin. Remove, delete, erase and destroy all interfaces with shadow selves and artificial intelligence, programs, patterns and records, all operating instructions, operating systems and operating programs that drive Magical Child Syndrome. Remove all recreator, reactivator, regenerator, and reinstaller viruses. Put them in the trash bin. Burn and incinerate them now. Thank you for your help. I am loving and forgiving myself now for giving up control of my life. I am taking back control and reclaiming my personal Power.

Step 19 Release Artificial Intelligence (AI)

This has more influence than I initially realized, and could explain why so many people have conflicts and problems in their life. I had assumed that it was basically just autopilot, but it is a totally separate operating system that functions with autopilot and MCS. If a person is a victim or has a hard time taking control of his life, AI will be the operating system that is controlling that person's life. We have found that in people who have compulsive behavior addictions to anything, AI will be the operating system with control over their life. If a person is in total denial of his behavior and refuses to acknowledge an addiction, you know that AI has control. Check 'no perception of denial files'.

AI can become the basic operating system for the Conscious Mind and will make decisions and function as a person's Conscious Mind. It has a duplicate set of programs identical to Conscious Rational Mind and can make decisions for you without your knowledge or control. If it is in control for an extended period, it can become an alternate personality. Deleting the operating system so that Conscious Mind can be reconnected to true self may take some hard work.

I have found that people who have given up control over their life numerous times are being controlled by Artificial Intelligence (AI). This operating system functions from Inner Conscious Mind. Sometimes it is working through Inner Middle Self, as well. If a person has made numerous attempts to learn about and try to reclaim their personal power in order to function better in their life, but they default and fall back into autopilot, then AI will take over. It does not let go very easily if it has had to pick up the pieces and reconstruct a person's life so they can function again. This is true of people who have had severe or prolonged depression or become victims of circumstances and given their power away to a group or a cult type organization. I have had to fight with this operating system to get it to let go many times. Victim programs must be addressed. Sometimes it will stop a person from making a proper decision to go off autopilot, or make a person sick to stop them from reclaiming to take their power back.

Usually, AI will not take over unless a person has given up their power to autopilot and refuses to take responsibility for their life. AI works in the background with autopilot, but if a person gives up and gets disoriented, confused, avoids responsibility, procrastinates and gets lost in a feeling of futility and indecision, it will come forward and take over. This is a crucial survival mechanism. In many cases, if a client has gone to many workshops and seminars looking for a way out, trying to use the processes and then giving up, AI will take over. If this happens too many times, the client will be debilitated and we will have a fight on our hands to get control back because AI will not believe that the client will take responsibility again, as they have given up too many times. AI will act as if it is a split personality in the way it controls a person's life. If it operates in this manner for an extended period, it will create a split personality or even multiple personalities if a person allows attached possessive beings to take over such as in bipolar or schizophrenia. It does not give up very easily once it has been in control many times. We must reason with it and let it know what our intentions are before it will let go and suspend autopilot. Check to see if there are multiple files, as sometimes, if a person has lost control many times and has exited into MCS numerous times, there may be more than one *AI* program operating. Ask:

"Is Artificial Intelligence operating at this time? Is it operating on autopilot? Are there multiple files?"

Affirmation to release Artificial Intelligence:
"In accordance with universal law free choice. I am asking you, Artificial Intelligence, to work with me. I know I gave up my personal power, responsibility and control in the past and let autopilot take over my life. I appreciate that you were able to help me survive and handle my life. I know now that it is my responsibility to take control back now. It is now my intention to reclaim my personal power to take responsibility to work through my issues. I am making a commitment to discipline and take control over my life now. I am asking you to remove autopilot and release your control now. I am asking my Higher Self, file and program manager to *uninstall the autopilot's operating system* and remove the interface which is operating artificial intelligence now and put it in the archives. Delete, erase and destroy all the programs, patterns, records, operating programs, instructions, systems, and all the recreator, reinstaller, reactivator, and reproducer programs that can reconstruct and reinstall the format that controls and operates autopilot now. Put them in the trash bin now. I thank you for your help. I am loving myself and forgiving myself for abdicating control of my life now."

Step 20: Remove Shadow Selves

The shadow self was first described by Carl Jung in the 1920s. His research on what was driving a person to sabotage himself and turn to negative behavior discovered the *shadow self*, the negative side of our personality self. It identifies with negative influences and is attracted to dark energies or dark forces. It may actually be spawned by the need to suffer. He felt this was a disowned sub-personality that was not discernible at the conscious level.

In my research, I have found that the shadow self operates from anger, rage, resentment, revenge, control, frustration, feelings of futility and feeling invalidated by family and society. This sub-personality wants attention but does not know how to get it in a normal manner. If it feels it is being ignored and taken advantage of, it strikes out in anger to get even. It is the self righteous warrior/fighter that holds on to resentment and seeks revenge.

Most people do not identify with this sub-personality or this aspect of the mind, which is why Jung described it as a disowned self and a shadow self. Its proclivity is to direct us to negative reactions and work with the negative aspects of self. He taught that this is the level of the mind and the mind set from which criminals operate. When it takes over and controls a person's behavior, it develops into a criminal personality.

My feeling is that shadow selves are located in the part of the mind that attracts the dark forces that plague us. I have added it to the list of basic sub-personalities as we find it in everybody. It must be removed from our operating system as it is not a supportive sub-personality similar to Critical Parent. The challenge is to recognize the path we are taking and the sub-personalities with which we identify our behavior. We have found multiple shadow selves in all our operating systems including regenerator viruses in the back-up files. If we have identified with negative interpretations or attitudes for any length of time, they have multiplied shadow selves. We must check all files and operating systems.

In general, the *"I have to suffer and struggle"* programs are hidden in shadow selves. They operate out of the denial files covered by shadow self. Programs can control your life with the help of autopilot.

We have also found that the shadow self will be activated by traumatic experiences where fear or anger is present automatically. We cannot afford negative attitudes or feelings, as they will break down our immune and endocrine systems and install shadow selves very easily.

In a client session, ask:

"Are shadow selves operating in the mind now? How many are in the file now? Are there any in back-up files with recreator, reactivator, regenerater and reinstaller virus programs attached?"

Affirmation to remove Shadow Selves:

"In accordance with universal law of free will and the law of right action, I am asking My Higher, file and program managers to capture, quarantine and remove an *infinity number* of shadow self sub-personalities from Conscious, Middle Self, Subconscious Mind, denial and no perception of denial-of-denial files, past, present, current, and future and parallel time-line files, back-up files and *an infinity number* of recreator, regenerator, reactivator, reinstaller virus programs that are responsible for rebuilding, reestablishing, reproducing and restructuring any relevant files and put them all in the trash bin. *Uninstall the operating systems*. Remove, delete, erase and destroy all the programs patterns and records, operating instructions, operating programs, operating systems and interfaces that shadow self operates from. Remove, erase, delete, and destroy all interfaces and all cellular memory imprints that pull undesirable people, events and external hostile forces to me which do not serve my best interests. Lock them up and send them to the trash bin. Burn and incinerate all files now. I thank you for your help. I am loving myself now."

Step 21: Remove Need to Suffer, Struggle, and be Punished

When an embryo is developing in the womb, it is the center of its universe and, provided the mother is not attempting to abort the child, all its needs are met. If the mother rejects the child in utero before birth, the rejection will deposited into cellular memory, developing into programs and locking "I am not accepted and I will suffer" into the files. How the child is treated after birth will govern how many "I need to suffer" programs are created. The modern birth process and sterile medical procedures cause terror and trauma which are not easily remedied without releasing the birth trauma. The young human goes from total megalomania to hapless, totally dependent victim in a relatively short period of time. The trauma establishes the *perception* in the child that trauma and suffering are the inherent nature of life in the physical realm.

This scenario warps or wounds the child's concept of who it is, and the Inner Child decides at some point to recapture its autonomy by reshaping its need to suffer on its own terms. It reasons that if it must suffer, *it* will determine the nature and extent of the suffering, which leads to self-damage that cyclically cripples life's potentials and destroys self-esteem, self-worth and confidence. If allowed to grow with the child, the longer it manifests in the child's mind, the more it destroys self-confidence, self-acceptance and self-esteem.

Over the last 20 years, we have seen amazing recoveries with the use of the this affirmation. We have found that over 99% of clients have these "I must suffer and need to be punished" programs. Much of this comes from the religious dogma that we are born in sin. I realized that many religious people will discount and negate our findings on this subject but we have found it to be locked into the mind in over 99% of clients, regardless of their religious views. How much influence the church, society and cultural models have on a person determines the number of "suffering" programs. If you feel rejected by God, quite often you will feel the need to be crucified to win God's love and acceptance. Churches, especially the Roman Catholic Church, orthodox churches and many conservative Episcopalian churches teach that suffering and martyrdom are the path to heaven. If you get caught up in the need to follow the lead of Jesus Christ, you will develop a need or want to be crucified program to be like him.

Many people may view this illusionary concept as a violation of God's laws so don't expect this perverted logic to make sense at the conscious level. It is the 'hidden agenda' that is created by interpretation and belief that not only manifests based on one's *interpretation* of the world but prevails as a program in the mind. These beliefs are foisted on us by our adult caregivers, and we accept their viewpoint as true. The Subconscious Mind accepts these concepts and creates programs based upon them, which must be reprogrammed to promote health, wealth, joy, happiness, safety and a secure sense of fulfillment. Suffering is not the path to enlightenment or abundance.

Using NK, check for each "I need to suffer" program, "I need to struggle," "I need to be punished," and "I need to crucified." (The latter is quite rare.)

Use the following affirmation to remove the client's need to suffer, struggle, to be punished.

Affirmation to remove need to suffer, struggle, to be punished:

"In accordance with universal law of free choice and right action, I am asking My Higher Self, file and program manager to remove an *infinity number of* :
- I have to suffer, struggle, to be punished,
- I need to suffer, to struggle, to be punished,
- I must suffer, to struggle, to be punished,
- I really must suffer, to struggle, to be punished,
- I want to suffer, to struggle, to be punished,
- I deserve to suffer, to struggle, to be punished,
- I must suffer due to guilt, cultural or race prejudice
- I must suffer, to be punished—to be crucified for karmic programs and contracts.

Remove them from Conscious, Middle self and Subconscious Mind's files, denial, no perception of denial-of-denial files, past, present, current, future and parallel time-line files, all back-up files. Capture, quarantine and remove <u>an infinity number</u> of recreator, regenerator, reactivator, re-installer virus programs and put them in the trash bin. *<u>Uninstall all operating systems</u>*, remove, delete, erase, destroy all programs, patterns, records, operating instructions, programs and systems that interface with any need to suffer programs. Burn this information in the incinerator. Destroy all interfaces with artificial intelligence and/or magical child syndrome. Erase, delete, destroy all ghost images and cellular and memory imprints, physical, emotional and all interfaces that attract people or situations to me that have contributed to or created suffering. Put them in the trash bin, burn and incinerate all files now. I thank you for your help, I am loving and forgiving myself."

Step 22: Remove the Traumatic Birthing Programs

For over 100 years medical doctors, have used a violent method to bring children into this world. Prior to the 1920s, most children were delivered by midwives. The medical profession tried to get midwives removed from delivering babies, claiming they could not handle an emergency. They believed births should be done only in hospitals.

According to Dr. Federick Leboyer, we must bring children into this world in the most loving, supportive method possible to avoid any possibility of physical shock to the body, traumatic rejection, and fear. To do this, we must reproduce the conditions and environment that exist in the womb until the baby is able to adjust the outside environment. In this manner, the baby adjusts to the conditions slowly and comes to life normally, breathing on its own, opening its eyes and smiling. To do this, the baby must be handled carefully and put in a basin of 98 degree water, or better, into a special bathtub.

The baby is left in the water until it adjusts to the environment and until the umbilicus stops pulsing. Then it is placed on the mother's chest so it can bond with its mother. If the umbilicus is severed before it stops pulsing, the baby feels as if it is suffocating. When it is cut, the baby is placed back in the water to wash it, then wrapped in a towel and replaced on the mother's chest. At this point, the baby will begin nurse automatically. They need the colostrum from the first nursing to build their immune system. Such a procedure makes the baby feel, "I am loved, wanted, accepted." Also, it bonds with the mother and feels her love.

When the baby is being expelled into bright lights and a cold, noisy room, it feels traumatized. This is a shock when the baby has been in a dark, warm, quiet totally protected environment for nine months. For some reason medical doctors think they must slap the baby on the bottom to get it to start breathing. This does not make sense since birth without violence has proven this concept false. The first five minutes of a child's life will set up programs of "I am being punished for something I have no awareness of and why?" How did you feel when you were held by your feet upside down and had your bottom slapped to force you to wake up and start breathing? It is traumatizing at least. Almost every adult alive today was birthed in this primitive manner. How does a baby react when subjected to tragic, fearful, terror-creating behavior by the very people who are supposed to help them enter in this new world? They start out life mistrusting adults, feeling they will be abusive to them.

The following affirmation usually brings up emotion, which shows us how traumatic this experience is. Seldom will any process release the feelings of fear, rejection and terror without using this affirmation.

Affirmation to release traumatic birth experience:

"I recognize now that I was subject to a violent traumatizing birthing experience that caused me to feel I was being suffocated from cutting my umbilical cord before I was ready to breathe, then being slapped to force me to breathe. This caused me to feel I was being punished for something I have no knowledge about. This destroyed my self-esteem, self-worth and self-confidence, causing me to feel I could not trust adults. I recognize now that I was not able to bond with my mother after birth. I am forgiving and releasing any resentment that I hold against my mother, as I know now it was not her fault. She had no control over the circumstances. I am releasing the doctors and nurses and midwives, loving and forgiving them, knowing that, in their ignorance and lack of knowledge, they did not know they were causing a terrifying experience for me which caused fear, disorientation and resentment toward adults. I am giving them 100% full permission to forgive themselves for the harm and trauma they inflicted on me. I am asking My Higher Self, and file and program managers to remove this file from all operating systems in Conscious Mind and Subconscious Mind and the Subconscious Mind's history archive files. I know now I can recover my self-esteem, self-worth and self-confidence. I know I can succeed at anything I choose to do now. I am loving myself and forgiving myself now."

Step 23: Installing Virus Quarantine Program and Firewall

We have a variety of virus protection programs such as Norton and McAfee for our desktop computers and I decided we needed the same protection for our mind. All programs and beliefs that cause breakdowns in our body/mind are virus-based. We identify these as programs that have an immediate effect on our health and well being.

Affirmation to install firewall and virus quarantine program:

"I am asking My Higher Self, File and Program Manager to create a firewall system to block installation of negative virus programs that will affect me or my mental emotional and/or physical health in any manner. Install this firewall in all operating systems. Install a quarantine program in all operating systems to scan all files for incoming virus programs that will have an adverse effect on health, wellness and well-being when they are activated and/or sent to any operating system in my mind. Set this up so it cannot be shut down or blocked by any outside source that may attempt to control me in any way.

"Set this program up to automatically capture, quarantine and delete all virus files when they are activated, before they are installed in Conscious or Subconscious Mind or any other operating system in my mind and send them to the trash bin. Lock them up and send them to the incinerator now. Thank you for your help."

Step 24: Clear Recycle Bin and Archive History Files:

Since our mind is running 24/7, it picks up files daily from all forms of sensory input including our thoughts, attitudes, feelings and what people say to us. Radio, TV, written material from magazines, newspapers and e-mails from your computer will be picked up randomly. This affirmation should be read at least once or twice a week or even daily if you find yourself picking up active files. This is the same function we use to clear the files on your desktop or laptop computer to clear the recycle bin, the archive files and the temporary Internet files. Your mind does not delete files unless you ask it to.

When we found this file, it was a bit mind-bending, in that our mind could have such a storage capacity that could be accessed so easy. The file space is unlimited as far I have found in our work. Our mind archives information and beliefs and programs just as our desktop or laptop computer we have today. It makes real sense. Your computer tracks every program you run, every file you access, every website you visit, and every e-mail you receive, and puts it all in temporary cache files or archive files. When you fill up your hard drive and do not have enough disc space to operate your computer properly, you must delete some files to free up space. When you delete all the temporary and archived files, you then have enough disk space for the computer to operate again.

Our inner computer seems to have unlimited space for storage of files and folders from every past life and all sensory input from this life, and keep them current and backed up every day. Since our mind backs up files daily, it will take the unused files and put them in the history archives, but they can be activated any time your file or program managers need to access them. (Attached beings love playing with these files and fouling up our life, too.)

Our Mind will only clear the files we ask it to delete and erase at any time. If we do not know these files exist or how to clear them, they can cause considerable problems for us. If we have programs that are setting us up to feel victimized, afraid of failure or success, afraid to ask for help, feel alone, unloved, or guilty, rejected and abandoned, and any of the hundreds of program files we have collected over the centuries, our mind can access them as it searches the data base for a method to handle a conflict or an emotion that has arisen. If they get installed and activated, they will create a physical reaction in the body. Good examples of this are asthma, allergies and even diabetes. We used these programs to get attention as a child, but we have no need for them as an adult so they were sent to the archives. When the same catalyst or trigger was activated by a similar emotion they were activated and moved to the active file and the condition is reactivated again.

This has happened to many people I have worked with, including myself, and we could not figure out how they were installed. When we found the back-up files, we figured we had the answer. But not so. We could delete and erase the online files, but we were not aware that there was another file in the history archives. We assumed that the only files in the history section were past lives.

I discovered the history archive files while waiting in the Salt Lake City airport due to a four hour layover because the earlier flights were over-booked. I decided I would use the time to work on my book on my laptop. My nose started bleeding and I was unable to stop it. It was bleeding as it did when I was a child, and I could not stop it sometimes for hours. In the bathroom, while trying to stop the flow, I went through every file I could think of. After twenty minutes, I came up with the history archive files. As soon as I discovered this file, I deleted and erased it and the bleeding stopped immediately.

Now that we can delete all files in the recycle bin and history archives, we will eliminate any programs from being activated in the future. This could be the answer to adult onset diabetes, herpes, allergies, hepatitis, all these mystery viruses and many more disease syndromes. I also have discovered that if the files become activated, they are reinstalled in many of the operating systems, which is the cause for these reactivated childhood illnesses and diseases. With this in mind, we must clear all the program files in the operating systems for any reactivated program and in the Subconscious Mind's history archive files.

Obviously this is the key to total healing. Now that we have the formula and can trace all programs to their source, we can clear them permanently. It is the key to being able to access all the files in the Subconscious Mind's database. It is much larger than I ever thought it was 15 years ago.

I theorized 20 years ago that Subconscious Mind or lower self had about 85% control over our life. Now I find it is quite reversed from that, and that Conscious Mind has 100% control over our life. That does not mean our true self has control, but that whoever is running your computer in Middle Self has control. All the operating systems that make up our Conscious Mind have control over our life until we take it back. When take responsibility and reclaim our personal power, and eliminate all the interlopers in our mind, we will have control. Until then the committee of personality selves and artificial intelligence will have control, plus any attached being they have invited in. If we have attached beings in our files playing games with us from split or multiple personalities, they can go right into these files and activate any one they choose and play it out. I have plenty of examples of this from my own experience.

Attached beings would get in me and activate these programs from time to time, so I have been bothered for the last 20 years by occasional health flare-ups from these programs. The closer we came to finding the cause, the more intense the flare-ups became. In the period October 2002 to April 2003, it would happen daily. Once we had removed all the split personality programs and the multiple personality selves, I assumed they would all be gone, but not so! There were hidden split personalities operating under names other than my given name. Since we removed all hidden split personalities and the files that were being activated, and installed a virus quarantine program and spam program, the flare-ups have stopped.

Repeat this affirmation at least twice a week for effective protection.

Affirmation to remove all files from Subconscious Mind's recycle bin and history archives, and set up and install Spam Blocker:

"I recognize that my mind sends all past life programs, unused programs, deleted and erased files to the recycle bin and the history archives in my Subconscious Mind. I recognize that when I do not want to deal with an issue, my mind will send files to denial or denial-of-denial. I am asking file and program managers to set up and install a *Spam Blocker program* to *capture and quarantine* all information that any authority figure says to me, or I hear from any person, radio and TV, or see or read from printed media. Remove any interpretations or perceptions about created attitudes, concepts, beliefs or programs that could or will have a negative effect on my happiness, my emotional, physical/mental health or well being. Capture and quarantine the beliefs, attitudes, concepts or programs immediately and remove them from my Conscious Mind's records before they enter my Subconscious Mind's data base. Remove all the files from Subconscious Mind's archives, back-up files, denial and denial-of-denial files. Send them to the trash bin so they will never affect me again.

"Do a file scan and a file search for all files and folders that contain programs, patterns, beliefs, concepts, interpretations, perceptions and attitudes that have been sent to the recycle bin, history archives, denial and denial of denial files. Remove all files, folders, and programs from the history archives, recycle bin, denial and denial of denial files. Send them to the trash bin.

"Remove all reduplicator, replicator, recreator, reactivator, reconstructor, reproducer and reinstaller virus operating instruction, systems and programs from the back up files send then to the trash bin.

"Remove the current and future time line files from Subconscious Mind, denial and denial of denial files and all operating systems in my mind so programs cannot be installed in them and lock them up. Put them in the trash bin so they will never affect me again. Empty the trash bin and send them to the incinerator now. Thank you for your help."

Step 25: Remove Authority Figure Program

This program gives your power away to authority figures. This is one of the most disconcerting programs. It was installed as an indigenous program in our mind at birth so we would give allegiance to our parents and follow their guidance as a child. As an adult, it has zero value as it causes us to give our power away to anybody who we think knows more about a subject than we do. It could be the plumber, garage mechanic, doctor or lawyer. If a doctor gives us a diagnosis of an illness, even if we do not have it, we will accept their diagnosis and we manifest the symptoms. We may even pick up something from what we read, hear or see if we give our power away to the authority behind the statement. These external opinions may internalize as a belief and will control our life. Programs which begin to operate from these files can annoy us because we do not know how to change them.

In a client session, ask:

"Is there an Authority Figure program operating in the mind now?"

Affirmation to remove the Authority Figure program:

"In accordance with universal law of free choice, I am asking file and program managers to capture, quarantine and uninstall the authority figure program. I realize it had value when I was a child so that I would follow my parent's guidance. As an adult, it has zero value as it causes me to give my power away to any person whom I recognize as an authority figure. Take this program out of all files and _uninstall the operating system._ Put it in the trash bin now. Delete, erase and destroy all the operating instructions, operating programs, patterns, records and systems. Put them in the trash bin so they will never affect me again. Delete, burn and incinerate all the files. Thank you for your help. I am loving and accepting myself now."

Step 26: Check for Negative Thought Forms

The most difficult traits to let go of are judgment, blame and resentment because we always want to believe that someone "did it" to us, which is convoluted reasoning. Nobody does anything to us that we do not ask them to do to us. At some level of our mind, we have invited people into our life to teach us lessons, but then we get angry at the teacher instead of thanking them for the lesson they brought to us. As a result, we destroy ourselves by getting angry at a lesson bearer that could have increased our level of enlightenment.

In a client session, ask:

"Are there any negative thought forms?"

If so, use the following affirmation.

Affirmation to clear Negative Thought Forms:

"In accordance with universal law of free choice, I am now releasing an *infinity number* of negative thought forms that have been inflicted on me by other people now. I am returning them to the originators. I do this with kindness and caring and unconditional love. I am releasing all self-inflicted negative thought forms with unconditional love and kindness and caring and I am doing that now. I am asking file and program managers to delete, erase and destroy all the operating programs, patterns and records and put them in the trash bin. Burn and incinerate them now. I am loving myself and forgiving myself and releasing myself from this bondage now. Thank you for your help."

Step 27: Check for Vows, Oaths, Allegiances and Vows of Poverty

In a client session, ask:

"Are there any previous vows, oaths or allegiances?"

If so, use the following affirmation.

Affirmation to release Vows, Oaths and Allegiances:

"In accordance with universal law of free choice and the law of right action, I am rebuking, revoking, renouncing, removing and releasing all vows, oaths and allegiances. I am asking file and program managers to capture, quarantine and remove an *infinity number* of vows, oaths and allegiances past, present and future, and vows of poverty, from _____ **and put them in the trash bin. Delete, erase and destroy all programs, patterns and records operating instructions, operating systems and put them in the trash bin. Burn and incinerate them now. Thank you for your help. I am loving myself and forgiving myself now."**

Step 28: Releasing Curses, Hexes and Spells

In a client session, use NK to check for each category. If present, use the following affirmation.

Affirmation to release Curses, Hexes, and Spells:

"In accordance with universal law of free choice and the law of right action, I am asking file and program managers to capture, quarantine and *remove an infinity number* of curses, hexes and spells from _____ _____ that are affecting me now. I am returning them to the originators with peace, love and forgiveness. I am doing that now. Delete, erase and destroy all the operating instructions, operating systems and operating programs, patterns and records put them all in the trash bin. Burn and incinerate them now. Thank you for your help. I am loving myself and forgiving myself now."

Step 29: Correct the Defective Digestive Program

All people who are carrying excess weight are not digesting the food that they eat, except for the simple sugars from the food. If overweight people try to lose weight with a protein diet, they will be hungry all the time. When they eat sugar-containing food, hunger will be reduced. Before any weight reduction is attempted, the digestive program in the mind must be rewritten. If the love program is not present, the digestive program will be overwritten and blocked. If Instinctual Mind is activated, it will block the digestive program and disable it, leaving only the simple sugar program. The above programs must be rewritten before the digestive program can be installed.

The digestive program is controlled by the lack of love program. When we clear that without accessing all the files from rejection, abandonment, lack of acceptance and love, the lack of love program can reactivate.

In client sessions, ask:

"Is your body living on simple sugars?"

If yes, then the program must be erased and new program installed using the following affirmation.

Affirmation to install a healthy digestive program:

"In accordance with universal law of free choice, I am asking file and program manager to uninstall this defective, malfunctioning digestive program that does not allow me to digest protein, carbohydrates, fats, oils, fruits and vegetables. I recognize that I am not assimilating the nutrients from the food I eat. Delete, erase and destroy all the patterns and records, all the operating instructions, systems and programs. Put them in the trash bin. I am asking you to install a new digestive program now that allows me to digest proteins, fats, oils, carbohydrates, vegetable and fruits and assimilate the nutrients for perfect health now. I am asking you to install this program in all files now so they will not be tampered with again. Thank you for your help."

Step 30: Remove the Aging Program

Due to the general acceptance that aging of the body is something we cannot stop, we accept that program, and our body breaks down with age. Aging is a state of mind that is controlled by our own programming and can be reversed. Pick a reasonable age where you felt good in your life and your body was healthy, and use it in the following affirmation.

Affirmation to remove the Aging Program:

"I recognize now that biological science, and most people, have accepted the aging of the physical body as inevitable and unstoppable. I know that, due to acceptance by society, I have accepted that aging of my body cannot be slowed down or stopped. This is a false and erroneous belief. I realize that this program can be removed from my mind and body. I am asking my file and program managers to capture, quarantine and remove this false operating program and system with all the operating instructions that indicate the aging of my body cannot be stopped. Lock them and seal them up and put them in the trash bin now so they will never affect me again. I am asking you to reinstall a new program that will cause my body to reverse the aging process. When I keep my health in perfect order with proper diet, exercise and supporting myself with positive mental input, my body will retain effective health I had at age ___."

Step 31: Installing "I Am Entitled To Money" and "I Can Receive Wealth" Programs

We never understood the importance of this affirmation until we began presenting seminars on accepting financial success. We all have a millionaire mind but it is so covered up with have not's and cannot's that we do not even know it exists. There are four types of people in our world:

1. *Losers*, who will never see the light of success as they do the daily drudge of low paying jobs and assuming this is their lot in life.

2. *Victim,* who sees everyone doing it to them. They are the victim of their own circumstances. Some of these people will see the light and pull up to the level of survivor.

3. *Survivors* have a chance to wake up and become winners because they push forward all the time even if they are carrying a heavy load. With some work, they can step in the winners' circle.

4. *Winners* are about 5% of the population. Being wealthy does not qualify a person to be in the winners' circle because there is more to wealth than money. Winning brings peace, happiness, harmony, joy, unconditional love and abundance. I have met many rich people who guard their money out of fear that they are going to lose it, which is not peace-of-mind. You cannot buy health and happiness with money; it is an inner sense of well-being.

Our first seminar on the Spiritual Psychology of wealth was an eye opener. Not one attendee at the seminar checked out positive for accepting money and wealth in their life. I told them that if there was a person who could receive a $100 bill, I would give it to them. Of course, every hand went up, but on checking with muscle testing, not one could receive it. Most people would find that odd. Why could you refuse to take a $100 bill. The catch is not, "Can you accept it?" but "Will your Subconscious inner programming allow you to accept it?"

We all have a millionaire mind but the catch is, can we find it? Most people cannot find it because it is so overwritten by the negative beliefs about money that they do not know that they are entitled to wealth. The following affirmation is the beginning of pulling out the hole of lack and loss, and describes all the different beliefs, concepts and interpretation we are holding about money, wealth and rich people.

This affirmation is written to allow your mind to release and let go of the dysfunctional software that is controlling your ability to accept wealth in our life. Every affirmation must be written in this way to reprogram and rewrite the script in our mind. Affirmations must acknowledge the negative (the software programming in our file now). Then we delete, erase and destroy the programs, patterns, records and operating instructions put them in the trash bin. Now we have an open file where can install a new effective program file that will support our transformation to a new reality. Not every person will have all the following programs, but rather than check for each one, we say them all as catch all.

This affirmation may require repetition to uncover all the programs from the mind's files. There could be past life files and many files from childhood, but it makes no difference if you do not have them all because we are deleting and erasing *all* of them in the following affirmation.

Affirmation to set up a positive money magnet:

"I recognize now that I am under the delusion and belief that I am not entitled to money, that I do not deserve money, that I am not able to accept wealth. Money is dirty. It is the root of all evil. Money doesn't grow on trees. We never have enough money so don't ask. Save your money for a rainy day you may need it. You must work hard for money. I can't keep money when I receive it. I don't want struggle and fight for money. Money creates pain and anguish. I must be very careful and guard my money or I will lose it. When I get money, someone is always trying to take it from me. I can't be happy without money so I will never be happy. Money is freedom and I can't keep money, so I will never have freedom from worry because I never have enough. Money can buy health and happiness but I never have enough so I will never be happy. I have money and it does not buy happiness because I am not happy, nor do I feel joy and peace. If I really tried to make money, I would fail so why try? Rich people are lucky; they always get the breaks. Spiritual people are not entitled to money. I do not want to be identified with those greedy grasping rich people.

"These are all false, erroneous beliefs, concepts and programs that I have accepted as true. In accordance with universal law of free choice and the law of right action, I am asking My Higher Self, and file and program managers to capture, quarantine and remove *an infinity number* of these false and erroneous programs, patterns, records, beliefs, concepts, attitudes and interpretations. Delete, erase and destroy all the operating instructions, systems, and programs. Put them all in the trash bin. Lock them up so they will never affect me again. Send them to incinerator and burn them now.

"I know now I am entitled to money. I can accept money, as I deserve money. I accept that spiritual people are entitled to wealth. I am entitled to wealth and riches of life. I can keep money, invest it wisely and benefit from my investments. Install this program in all the files now. Thank you for your help. I am loving myself and forgiving myself for holding these false and erroneous beliefs now."

Step 32. Install Creator Self

When we achieve the level of competency where we can be spiritual beings, this will work with no effort. But, if we are not at that level, no matter how many times we do this affirmation, it will not hold. It only works when we obtain the level evolvement and enlightenment.

Your mind will not allow you to go beyond your level of competence, so increase that level using the following affirmation.

Affirmation to install Creator Self program:

"I am asking you, Higher Self, file and program managers, to uninstall the operating systems' programs to block and limit my Divine Creator Self, the Presence of GOD within to activate the manifestation of my flight plan and GOD's divine plan in my life now. I realize I have been functioning as physical being having occasional spiritual experiences. I am asking you to capture, quarantine and remove <u>an infinity number</u> of programs, patterns and records that disempower, sabotage, or block the manifestation of my flight plan and GOD's divine plan in my life. Delete, erase and destroy all programs, patterns, records and their operating instructions and put them in the trash bin.

I now give permission to my Divine Creator Self to set up and conform me to the image of the Christ Master Self. I know now I can be a spiritual being having physical experiences *now*. I am doing that now. Thank you for your help. I am loving and forgiving myself now."

Step 33: Release unidentified programs and files

Programs may often pop up that seem to have no connection with any form or situation that is recognizable. For example, my foot began to itch for no reason. When I checked, I found it was an old athlete's foot program from the past. These programs are usually attached to a saboteur recreator, reactivator or a virus program that has been installed by a saboteur sub-personality.

Many times these programs are activated by old childhood programs that were shoved out of the way, suppressed and locked in denial or denial-of-denial files. If you have a habit pattern that you have overcome, it may be sitting in wait to spring up on you when you least expect it. The program is locked in the files unless it has been released and rewritten.

Quite often, when we feel tired but have not worked really hard or have not been under stress, we will feel as if we need to get some sleep, and end up taking a nap. This is caused by mental blocker or energy blocker programs. At times when we are confronting a new issue or new direction in our life, our mind may make us sleepy to avoid following through with the project. This happened to me many times when I was starting a new project. By simply releasing the mental blockers, you will be back on track wide awake.

I have discovered childhood illnesses reactivate 30 to 40 years after they disappeared in teenage years. When we go through a reaction/emotion that is a similar experience from the past, an activator or catalyst attached to the program reinstalls the program in an active file. The cause and core issue were never released, so it just became a dormant program. When it reappears, we can release it very easily.

Just overcoming a negative habit by will power or discipline will not erase and delete a program or file. You must be able to locate and describe the program before our mind will delete and release it. The program or file must be brought up and identified to make sure you have an exact match, or the program will not be erased and deleted. Visualization will sometimes remove a program temporarily, but it very seldom will actually delete the file.

The most effective way is to ask Higher Self, file and program managers to perform a file scan and file search for the file or program. When it is identified, delete it from all files with the following affirmation. If you know which operating system it is in, all you must do is delete it from that system.

Affirmation to release unidentified files and programs:

"I am asking you, Higher Self, and file and program managers, to capture, quarantine and remove <u>an infinity number</u> of: _____.

"Remove all the programs, patterns, records, operating instructions from Conscious and Subconscious Minds' operating files, back-up files, time-line files, denial and denial-of-denial operating files. Put them all in the trash bin, lock them up and send them to the incinerator so they will never affect me again and burn them now."

Use this affirmation if the programs keep coming up again and are repeatedly being installed.

"I am asking Higher Self, file and program managers to perform a file scan and a file search for recreator, duplicator, regenerator, reactivator, reconstructor and reinstaller virus programs in all files and operating systems. Uninstall all operating systems capture and quarantine and remove <u>an infinity number</u> of these files, programs and patterns. Put them in the trash bin. Delete erase and destroy all files and put them in the incinerator and burn them now."

Step 34: Rebalance polarity and integrate new programs

At the end of each session, recheck the "need to suffer" (NTS) quotient (on a scale of 1 – 10) bilaterally (using both arms at the same time). If equal on both sides of the body, then all of the programs that are activated have been released. If the body is weak on one side, then more work is indicated on either fear, anger, resentment or responsibility. This does not mean that all programs have been cleared, as many could locked into denial-of-denial. The level that was cleared will allow an older layer to move up. As with peeling an onion, one layer will reveal the next layer of programs. The intent is to reduce NTS to zero.

Step 35: Clean up

Make sure that all programs, beliefs and sub-personalities that were sent to the trash bin are deleted, put in the incinerator and burned.

In Conclusion

This book (Book One) is the first step in the process of Psychoneuroimmunology. Energy Psychology is the process of locating the dysfunctional programs. Beliefs will be only in the mind's database programming. If they are held for a period of time and traumatic experiences are attached to them, they will move to the body as evidenced by the Body Map diagrams in Appendix B of this manual.

Release of cellular memory is the next step in the process, that of Energy Medicine. This is explained in my book *Your Body Is Talking; Are You Listening?* and in the training manual for module one of the Energy Medicine/Energy Psychology training in the course on Psychoneuroimmunolgy.

Book Two in this series will be on Energy Medicine—removing the blocks from cellular memory. Our body is our mind; the physical extension to mind is our body. Programs that are traumatic in nature will be deposited in our body and appear as pain. We cannot avoid the lesson as it will become so evident that nothing will stop the pain. Every symptomatic form of relief will eventually become ineffective at releasing the pain. The only way to permanently remove and clear the pain is removing from cellular memory in the body the programs, habit patterns and the operating instructions that are causing the pain.

We all have the opportunity to become successful in our lives. The question is, are we going to take the bull by the horns and ride him? Who is the bull? We are, but we must understand that we must take control and tame our out-of-control mind that has caused our us to lose control of our life.

We must recover our lost self. Many people seem to get on track and succeed yet along the line, somehow they trip over their own issues because they have not worked them out. Why is it they were on the track to success and then stumbled? In November 2004, I discovered the cause. Most people have special relationships with themselves they are not aware of. I addressed this situation in Step 18 of chapter 10. My discovery that it was the illusion that we run our life with answered many questions I had about people who assumed they had nothing major to deal with in their life. Many of these illusions are around status, and the need for control, validation and acceptance. These people would appear to be successful in their life in one or two of the four quadrants, yet when we dig deeper into their lives, we find dysfunctional programs that are holding them back from total wellness. The other side of these special relationships are people who victimize themselves by trying to get validation by being rescuers, saviors or empathizers. These people try to get acceptance by giving and helping, in hopes that they will be recognized by the receiver for their giving and helping.

All of these special relationships will keep us from total wellness as we are living in an illusion we cannot perceive. When an observer questions our behavior, we will jump to justify what we have done or who we are, to defend our position. Quite often, we will resort to projection, trying to take the focus off ourselves and pointing our remarks to the person we feel is criticizing us.

Success can be a hard lesson if you focus on money and position without building a solid foundation. A shaky foundation will crumble and it could cause a meltdown and a major physical breakdown. Such people would not be considered winners, even though they had achieved success on a financial level. This is only one of the tracks on the path to wellness as a total state of being.

When we overcome our special relationship with ourselves, we can step into the winners' circle. It takes real courage, conviction and commitment to discipline ourselves to walk through the veil of illusions that cover our shortcomings and block us from total wellness and success.

Why do winners seem to have to have the "Midas Touch" such that everything they do *turns up roses?* There is not just one factor. Most successful people have stumbled at some point in their life, but they pick themselves up and do not look back in anger, fear or resentment. *They forge on, knowing that was just a bump on the path and they are past it now. It was a lesson in reclaiming their personal power and taking control of their life path. Once they have done it, they know they can do it again.*

When we do an overview of an individual's life, we are evaluating all four tracks on the path to wholeness:
1. Physical health, diet, exercise, and nutrition
2. Mental health, emotional, psychological and relationships
3. Financial health, success and abundance
4. Spiritual health, evolution, enlightenment, transformation and connection with GOD/higher power

They all must be in line and built on a strong foundation or somewhere along the path we will experience a meltdown, with a physical breakdown as the end result.

Contact Information

Workshops on the Energy Medicine-Energy Psychology and Neuro/Cellular Repatterning are presented every month in many cities in the U.S. and Canada.

- For information about workshops and programs, or for a list of practitioners, email us at: energypsychology@mindspring.com
- For information about the process in this manual go to: www.transformyourmind.com
- For books, go to: www.personaltransformationpress.com
- For information about the StressBuster, go to: www.StressBuster.org

We will begin the one-year internship training program in January 2005. This will be a course on training in Energy Medicine, creating a life that supports your ability to function at a high level of success with peace, happiness, harmony, joy and an abundance of unconditional love and financial security. The major stumbling block for most people is the Fear Factor. When we break through the fear barrier, we can succeed at levels that make you to wonder why you did not find this long ago.

We will also focus on marketing yourself and products, building functional businesses that can return significant income to you that you are entitled to. We will also set up a program for service to others. What you give you receive in return.

You can enter the program at any time, and your one-year internship begins when you enter the program. The fee for internship training will be $7,797. For more information, email us or visit our website.

You can receive a $ 2,000 discount by paying in full on entering the training program.

If you have attended our workshops before, the fee will be reduced by $1,000 for level 1, $1,500 for level 2. That's a total of $2,500 for both workshops.

The entry fee for the one year payoff is $597, with no interest charges.

Appendix A

How the Mind Functions

The human mind is a tool for transformation provided that we use it properly. Contrary to popular belief, there is more to our mind than brain researchers have found. Some psychologists divide mind into the Conscious and Unconscious minds. Others refer to the Subconscious Mind, which is the appropriate description because it is far from the dictionary description of the word "unconscious." It is on 24/7 and records in its database every form of sensory input that we allow in.

Our mind has a number of levels, distributed across Middle Self and Lower Self, each with specific duties to perform (see Figure A-1):

- Conscious Rational Decision-making Mind, where we operate from if we are in control of our life
- Autopilot and Inner Middle Self, which house a number of sub-personalities
- Subconscious Mind, database or memory.
- Ego, or file manager that gets and puts data to and from Subconscious Mind

The challenge is to get all levels aligned with each other so they have the same objective and same priorities to accomplish our goals in life. But seldom do I find people with all four systems aligned and operating together.

HIGH SELF
Connection to GOD Self. Akashic Record Telephone operator Connection to Source Mind and the Hall of Records

MIDDLE SELF
Conscious Rational Decision Making Mind Auto Pilot (Justifier, Judger sub-personalities) Inner Middle Self (Control, Manipulator sub-personalities) Instinctual Self, Survival Self

LOWER SELF
Subconscious Mind Ego Holographic Mind (Soul Mind)

Figure A-1: Levels of Mind

The Middle Self

Middle Self consists of five components (see Figure A-1):

- *Conscious Rational Decision-making Mind*, the functional aspect, the "keyboard" where you, the conscious self, program and control your life.
- *Conscious Mind Operating files:* The operating files that run your life on a day-to-day basis when you are in control of your mind's activities. If you are not in control, your mind goes on autopilot and Artificial Intelligence in Inner Middle Self.
- *Autopilot*, which can run your life without your control through Artificial Intelligence and all the sub-personalities in Middle Self's files. When people go on autopilot, they give their power away to a sub-personality that they created to escape from some situation or experience.

- *Inner Middle Self*, with Control and Manipulator sub-personalities: it will control all your behavior if you have given your personal power and control to autopilot. Artificial Intelligence (AI) is an operating system that operates through the inner mind's operating systems, and will control your life along with autopilot when you default on your attempt to regain control of your life and take your power back. It has an exact duplicate set of the file operating programs that are in the Conscious Mind so it can run our life without our support.

- *Survival Self/Instinctual Mind,* which operates out of the limbic part of the brain. Some people describe it as the animal or reptilian mind. Brain researchers theorize that this is the oldest part of the brain. I feel this could be inaccurate since its actions interleave with the actions of the Inner Middle Self, which operates from beliefs, concepts, interpretations and attitudes. These, if acted on over time, will create programs and patterns. It also has a set of sub-personalities for each concept or belief. These two are not active unless one goes into survival from a life-threatening illness. Since the events of September 11, 2001, I have found 95% of my clients are operating out of Instinctual Mind. Apparently, most people found this event so traumatic that it disoriented and confused them, and caused them so much fear that they did not know whether they wanted to live or die. Very few people are aware that this happened, so they are unaware to this day that they're living in survival. You, the reader, may be in survival mode right now, and operating from Instinctual Mind files.

The committee in your Middle Self is also in session 24 hours a day. It doesn't care if you listen in, since it feels that it operates quite well without you. If you are not making the decisions that affect you and are not taking responsibility for what happens in your life, your sub-personalities will make the decisions for you. They may not make the choices you would consciously make, but someone has to be at the helm all the time.

Autopilot and Artificial Intelligence may do a fine job of guiding you through your day if there are no crises or confrontations where you have to make decisions, but if a situation occurs that requires decisive action, someone has to make that decision. If you are not at the helm, your Inner Middle Self's irrational mind, your autopilot, and its committee will make your decisions for you.

Middle Self bases its action on how you have handled the situation in the past. It scans the files and, if no program exists, the committee will take whatever action best promotes its survival. If you are in a situation that, at a conscious level, you consider beneficial to you but which your committee of sub- personalities views as threatening, it will try to sabotage you.

If you are not in total control of your life, your Middle Self committee will try to stop any threat to its power. If you give it the message that you are claiming your personal power and taking responsibility for your life, it will readily relinquish its power to you. However, at first, it won't trust you, and you will have to prove yourself.

If you have defaulted on attempts to reclaim your personal power and take control of your life, Artificial Intelligence, which operates out of Inner Conscious Mind, will have taken over control of your life with autopilot. At this point, you will need to demonstrate your intention and commitment, or AI will not give up control very easy if you have defaulted in many attempts to take control of your life.

The Operation of the Mind

The process begins with receipt of sensory input, be it a sound, sight, smell or touch. However, the stimulus can also be a thought or memory, meta-communication, information from higher sources, and new thought forms. Figure A-2 shows how the mind routes information. Figures A-3 and A-4 show the results of the reactions and responses.

When our Conscious Mind records sensory input, it decides how it will react or respond, interprets how it feels about the incoming information, and places a feeling on it. It will either take responsibility and route the information to the Conscious Rational Mind, or make no decision and pass it on to Inner Conscious Mind and Middle Self. If we are making our own decisions on how to handle the situation, Middle Self routes the information

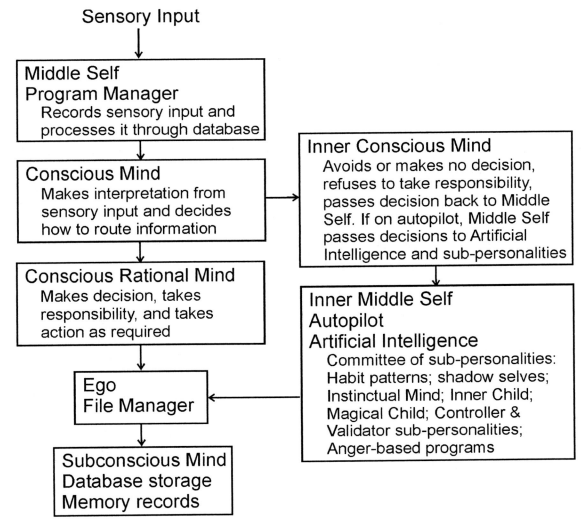

Figure A-2: How the Mind Routes Information

to Ego (file manager), which files it in Subconscious Mind's database. Ego can retrieve information from our database and return it to Conscious Mind for future use.

As we can see by Figure A-2, if we do not take responsibility, sensory input takes a totally different route through our mind. If we choose not to be in control, Artificial Intelligence runs our life quite well. The problem with this, however, is that we have no control about what action it takes. It could cause a stroke or heart attack to slow us down, or cause us to take notice of the people we are rejecting or avoiding. It can cause myriad illnesses and diseases to act out our fear or anger.

When we clear all the sub-personalities and the negative habit patterns, we can get control back. It takes some work to get the flow of information to run through our mind without being detoured through the sub-personalities. Figure A-2 shows how the mind routes the sensory input through the operating systems and Figure A-3a and A-3b showhow the mind responds or reacts to the sensory input and the effects it has on our behavior.

1. *Sensory input* (visual, auditory, physical feeling, meta-communication, and information from higher sources). and *new thought forms* (creative, inventive and intuitive), plus *processing dialogue* (negative or positive thought forms, flash back, memories, misinterpretations) are fed to the Middle Self.

2. *Middle Self interprets* the perceived information, processing through the Conscious Rational Mind or autopilot sub-personalities. (Middle Self and Subconscious Mind search for programs of past reactions or responses, and the operational program controls Reaction/Response.)

3. *Assignment of feeling:* Determines what action to take. At this point, you have two choices: Reaction or Response. Your choice is based on past belief or perceived effect from installed programs.

4. *Catalyst:* Loss of control pushes you into fear/anger, degenerating into emotional reaction and giving away your personal power.

5. *Unconscious Decision* is made in an instant based on Catalyst as to which action to take—flight or flight.

6. *Emotional Reaction:* No choice/ no decision, result in:
   a. *Flight/avoidance.* Run away from feeling;
   b. *Fight/confront.* Defensive, blowup out of control;
   c. *Defense of action.* Justification of action, denial feelings;
   d. *No reaction:* total avoidance with repression of feeling/emotion;
   e. Either *deny* or *wake up* to the lesson and review the situation that caused the reaction.

7. *Denial/Justification:* Falling back into the illusion of the past denial as a victim, justifying behavior as the only responsible reaction we could take. At this point, illusion and denial may form a denial-of-denial sub-personality, If this happens, the cause of the behavior is totally suppressed *as if it does not exist.* We can then assume that our reaction was an accurate truthful way to handle the situation.

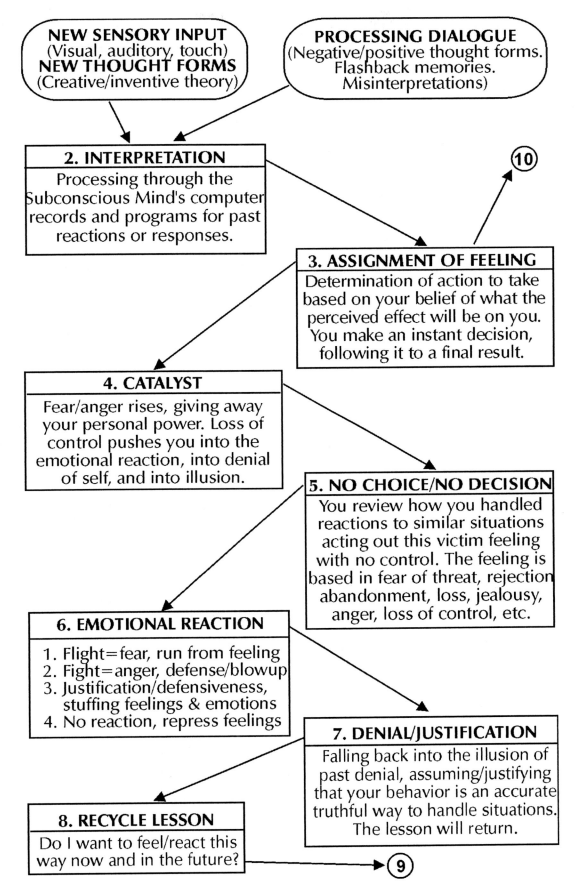

NEW SENSORY INPUT
(Visual, auditory, touch)
NEW THOUGHT FORMS
(Creative/inventive theory)

PROCESSING DIALOGUE
(Negative/positive thought forms.
Flashback memories.
Misinterpretations)

2. INTERPRETATION

Processing through the
Subconscious Mind's computer
records and programs for past
reactions or responses.

⑩

3. ASSIGNMENT OF FEELING

Determination of action to take
based on your belief of what the
perceived effect will be on you.
You make an instant decision,
following it to a final result.

4. CATALYST

Fear/anger rises, giving away
your personal power. Loss of
control pushes you into the
emotional reaction, into denial
of self, and into illusion.

5. NO CHOICE/NO DECISION

You review how you handled
reactions to similar situations
acting out this victim feeling
with no control. The feeling is
based in fear of threat, rejection
abandonment, loss, jealousy,
anger, loss of control, etc.

6. EMOTIONAL REACTION

1. Flight=fear, run from feeling
2. Fight=anger, defense/blowup
3. Justification/defensiveness,
   stuffing feelings & emotions
4. No reaction, repress feelings

7. DENIAL/JUSTIFICATION

Falling back into the illusion of
past denial, assuming/justifying
that your behavior is an accurate
truthful way to handle situations.
The lesson will return.

8. RECYCLE LESSON

Do I want to feel/react this
way now and in the future?

⑨

Figure A-3a: How the Mind Responds/Reacts to Sensory Input

8. *Recycle Lesson:* At this point, you may review your behavior and ask yourself, "Do I want to feel/react this way now and in the future?" If you can do this, you can recycle the lesson.

9. *Recognition of Denial:*
    a. Review behavior you deem as ineffective;
    b. Recognize the effect of the lesson;
    c. Move into recovery and erase the ineffective program and remove the sub-personality driving the program;
    d. Remove denial-of-denial sub-personalities if you can recognize them;
    e. Change the negative justifying reactions to positive responses;
    f. Rewrite a new program and install it in the files;
    g. Recognize that you create all lessons, so that you can shift from victim to cause;
    h. Love and forgive yourself for allowing this to happen.

10. *Choice/Decision:* When we recognize this decision point, we have about 30 seconds to detach from the emotion and respond in an effective way. State, "I choose to step out of denial, illusion and justification. I will not act out, repress, justify, manipulate, try to control or judge another's behavior."

11. *Response:* If we are not able to detach from the emotion immediately, we will go into recycle. If we can respond effectively and positively, we review the possible avenues and responses to handle the situation with acceptance, forgiveness and unconditional love. At this point, we can detach from the emotion and avoid separation from self.

12. *Denial Reaction* will take over due to our inability to maintain and control our response. Loss of control will push us into the emotion. We recycle the lesson again.

13. *Detachment:* Hallmarks of successful detachment are the ability to recognize the feeling with a new viewpoint and interpretation, and honestly say to ourselves:
    a. This is not an attack on my self-worth or who I am.
    b. I do not have or need authority or control over anybody.
    c. I can respond in a positive manner to every feeling or situation and all people at all times.
    d. I am all right under all conditions, in all circumstances, in all situations and at all times.
    e. My self-esteem and self-worth are unaffected by this experience.
    f. I can respond with love, kindness and forgiveness at all times.

14. *Transformation:* This occurs when we can recognize that we do not need control or authority at any time. We will not be attacked at any time, nor do we have to defend ourselves or attack back. When we release fear, anger, control, authority, judgment and justification, we have made it through the transfiguration, and unconditional love, peace, happiness, harmony and joy are our entitlement.

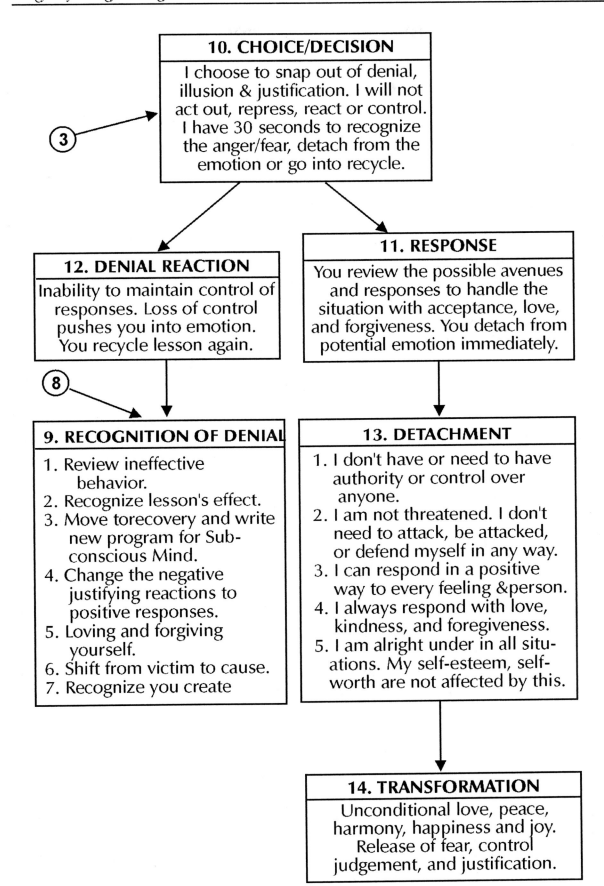

Figure A-3b: How the Mind Responds/Reacts to Sensory Input

Split Personalities

Sub-personalities are the driving force behind habit patterns. If you follow a certain action, belief or interpretation often enough, it will become a habit pattern. If you deny that you are following that pattern, it will become a denial sub-personality. If you persist in denying the program that the pattern created, you may become totally separated from yourself and move into denial of denial. If you disassociate from yourself at times of great stress, you become a split or multiple personality. At this point, the sub-personalities become who you are, as you become totally separated from self.

Most people with this dysfunction are labeled as psychotic or schizophrenic, a condition that may result in a possessive spirit walking in and taking over. At this point, people can leave for short times (a few minutes to hours), but sometimes, people leave for many years, with no recollection of what they have done or where they have been. This demonstrates the awesome power of the mind to operate without our approval or direction.

All mental dysfunction is caused by a choice by the mind to create another world to run away from some traumatic experience. Almost all dysfunction of this type starts with a childhood experience. The child will escape into an imaginary world that he or she sets up to avoid pain. I refer to this as "escaping into the Magical Child," which is controlled by the Inner Child sub-personality. This will be carried through life until it released.

People can also disappear when they go on autopilot and give their power away to another created sub-personality that was created to escape from some situation or experience. Middle Self sub-personalities can set up autopilot operating systems in the Conscious Rational Mind and, as a result, our life is run without our consent or control.

Figure A-4 portrays the formation of a split personality:

1. Sensory input from a trauma, pain, situation or any form of abuse will cause a person to escape into a magical child.

2. Middle Self creates a sub-personality to accommodate the escape.

3. Person goes on autopilot or has been on autopilot at times. This evolves into multiple sub-personalities that control the mind's functioning. The person and the original personality self shut down. Split personalities are a series of sub-personalities running a person life.

4. Multiple personality disorder and schizophrenia are generally caused by an attached spirit being taking over, becoming another personality self.

Summary of How the Mind Works

The brain is not the only part of the body that has the ability to think. Every cell has a limited ability to make decisions based on input by neuropeptides and cytokinins. Every organ and gland has receptors that communicate with the brain's switching network, and evaluate all sensory input as it comes in for interpretation for application.

The brain's switching network consults your mind's database for files from the past and decides how you will react or respond based on how you reacted in the past. Your mind interprets the feeling, which in turn causes a chemical reaction or response in the body at

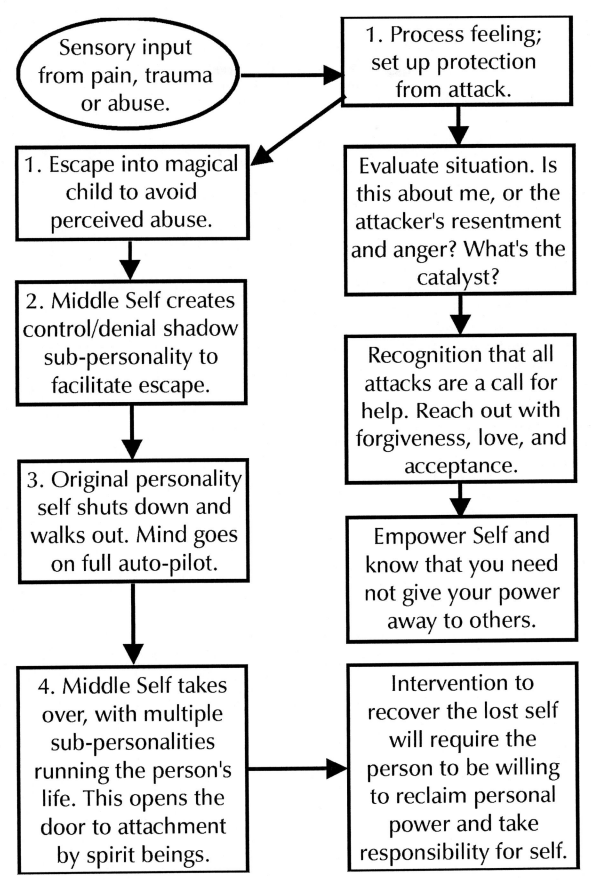

Figure A-4: Creation of a Split Personality

all levels. A positive feeling creates a positive response that sends supportive information to the cells, organs and glands, which in turn strengthens and builds health and wellness and a feeling of well-being. This feeling causes the release of the "happy" brain chemicals interlukins, seratonin, interferon, and L-Dopa, that in turn cause a feeling of peace, happiness, harmony, and joy.

Negative feelings, on the other hand, cause a chain reaction, shutting down the happy chemicals and sending negative reactions through the neuropeptides and cytokinins to the body at every level, which begins to suppress, depress and breakdown cellular structures in every cell, organ and gland. If the mind senses attack, it sets up a flight-or-flight syndrome. The immune and endocrine systems try to build a defense but are limited because they cannot counteract the negative thought form reaction that's being circulated throughout the body. The adrenals begin to pump all the time, creating adrenal overload as they try to support the body. The mind signals fear and stress, which cause the body to go into adrenal exhaustion trying to counteract the stress. If this continues to the point of adrenal exhaustion, it will cause depression.

If the Magical Child Syndrome is active and is triggered or activated, the personality self will shut down the Conscious Mind and disappear. Very seldom does one notice this happening as it is all internal. There is one exception to this reaction; those who are strong enough and have the willpower to stay in control can ward off the downer reaction for years. Eventually, the body will break down and the mind will crash the operating system, with traumatic results as the person will crash with depression or a serious illness.

Sub-personalities: Their Origin and Effect

Traditional Transactional Analysis works with five basic sub-personalities: Inner Child, Critical Parent, Survivor Self, Inner Adult, and Inner Self. These sub-personalities are the group that is in our mind's files from birth. They can have a major effect on your life and, if you operate on autopilot or give your power away to any of them, they will function *as you* and *for you*, projecting their agendas on your actions. Over the years, we discovered that the Personality Self is composed of more than 100 sub-personalities, along with all the mind's operating systems that drive them.

We have added another sub-personality to the basic five. Discovering the shadow self was another major breakthrough, for we discovered the sub-personality that creates conflict in our life. Shadow self works through and with Critical Parent, and focuses on criticism, negativity, anger, resentment, blame and rage, because it likes to stir up trouble, conflict and argument. Shadow self is the creator of compulsive/obsessive behavior patterns. It is also the cross-talker that is chattering in the back of our mind when we want to be quiet.

When we discovered that the mind is not limited to the basic five sub-personalities, we discovered that the Personality Self really runs our life, with its committee of 100 or more sub-personalities, each acting out a specific behavior trait. As we dug deeper into this, we discovered that Personality Self is what people have traditionally labeled Ego. As we expanded our knowledge of the concept, we found that we could change clients' personality traits, which changed their life path. People who were considered self-centered and egotistic would become more compassionate and supportive. Those who were nonassertive would move to a more assertive position and reclaim their personal power. Over time, we were able to show people how to reconstruct their personality so they would be more effective in their life. This is the goal of psychology but it does not work very well. It certainly didn't work for me, so I gave it up and began to search for a new approach.

The five basic sub-personalities are indigenous to our mind. This means that they cannot be deleted or destroyed, even though I would like to have done so many times. We must train the basic sub-personalities to work with us, and give us back control. As children, we needed their help to navigate through life but, as we grew up and learned to deal with life, they should fade into the background. However, they do not "fade away" when people do not take their personal power back from them, preferring to relinquish responsibility for their life.

In the past, sub-personalities were believed to be located in the Subconscious Mind, but in fact, they reside in the Middle Self and function autonomously, almost as a separate mind. It was also thought that the five were driven by Ego, which spawned the term "egotistical" because they do, at times, display what most people mean by the term "egotistical behavior." However, this is erroneous because Ego has no driving force that would cause it to act egotistically, nor can it recreate a sub-personality trait that is driven by the Controller, Justifier, Self-righteous, Competitor, Confronter, Know it all, Manipulator, Authority and Judger sub-personalities. The only part of mind that can create a sub-personality is Middle Self, which serves as Program Manager (see Figure A-5).

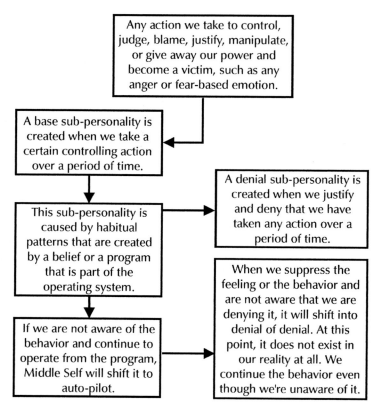

Figure A-5: Creation of Sub-personalities

When people are on autopilot, the sub-personalities run the body/mind on their own, having no real connection with Ego at all. The more we evaluated Ego, we more we found it to be simply a file manager for the database in Subconscious Mind's computer, serving as librarian, secretary, and file clerk. When we stopped confronting Ego as an adversary, it became friendly and helpful. We also discovered an interesting phenomenon: people's memories started getting better, proving that Ego was the file clerk for our memory. As we delved into this vast unknown area of the mind, we found that the makeup of the mind was as orderly and smooth-running as a computer running an operating system and programs that could be reprogrammed.

We believed that Middle Self was the area of the mind in which sub-personalities operated; at least, that was our impression until we ran into autopilot, which has sub-personalities that we create when we let autopilot run our life and refuse to take responsibility. Although it resides in Middle Self, autopilot operates from the Conscious Mind working through Artificial Intelligence. We found many sub-personalities, each driving a particular emotion or behavioral habit pattern. We also found that sub-personalities can drive beliefs, interpretations, feelings and programs. The more we evaluated the Personality Self, the more we found that all emotional behavior is caused by sub-personalities. Programs cause emotional behavior, but they must have sub-personalities to act out the emotional behavior.

People often blame the Inner Child for unruly behavior, and then deny that they have control over it. Many people in 12-Step recovery groups such as Codependents

Anonymous separate the Inner Child out as "not them" and then blame it for their emotional behavior. But Inner Child *is* part of us and we must get it to grow up and stop acting like a victim. The degree to which it will fight for control depends on how much power we have given to it. Most of the time, it is not working on its own but through the Magical Child Syndrome.

Survivor Self sees its role as protecting you, so it will sabotage you if it feels you are going the wrong direction. Critical Parent berates you for not doing an effective job, so that you reject yourself. Critical Parent is the most active in children because they feel they do not match up (due to rejection and parental expectations) and it spares no effort in validating any perceived shortcomings.

As you grow up, you create the Judger, Controller, Justifier, Manipulator, Competitor, Avoider and myriad anger and fear selves that run your life. And each time you run into a problem you cannot handle, your mind searches the database and may create another sub-personality to deal with it. If you encounter a habit pattern that you don't want to deal with and choose to delude yourself, your denial creates a denial sub-personality to justify your behavior and cover it up, so that you don't even understand what you are running away from. If you try to suppress the pattern totally, the sub-personality will create a "denial of denial" sub-personality to bury it completely. You will not even recognize the behavior pattern yet it is clearly visible to other people.

This cascade effect was one of the most significant causes of separation from self. When separation from self begins to take hold, an inner shadow sub-personality blocks the person from understanding this phenomena. The more we go into denial of separation from self, more inner shadow sub-personalities are created. I have removed up to 35 inner shadow sub-personalities that were feeding negative self-talk to a client.

Sub-personalities can be up to three deep on any one subject. Not only that, but dysfunctional programs and patterns often have a backup sub-personality. If these are not addressed, they will create a new program or belief to drive them. We once believed that we simply had to get to the core issue and the base cause. Now we realize that we must also check for sub-personalities. That was not all; each sub-personality has denial sub-personalities, with a backup for each.

The hardest sub-personalities to locate are "denial of denial." Unless you're willing to face the truth and go for it, dropping all of the illusions you operate from, and face the situations you are able to deal with, you cannot get to the denial sub-personalities. They are there for the very purpose of denial, so you will be blocked, making locating them very hard.

If you feel you have handled the situation when, in fact, all you did was suppress or release the feeling with a cathartic emotional discharge, then you put the issue into denial. The issue continues to be active except that it is suppressed and no longer accessible by your Conscious Mind. If the issue surfaces again and you do not clear it, then it goes into a "no perception of denial of denial" file. The more we deny behavior patterns and issues, the more we tell Middle Self that we do not want to take responsibility. This causes Middles Self to refer the issue to autopilot, which in turn creates more sub-personalities to handle our lives.

How the Mind Copes with Conflict

Figure A-6 shows that we can deal with conflict in our lives in one of two ways:

a) Defensive and closed, which leads to the intent to protect against anticipated pain and fear, or

b) Non-defensively and open, with the intent to learn from the conflict.

With low self-esteem, and self-worth eroded by a negative environment, our primary motivation is the avoidance of future pain. We employ three main pain-avoidance strategies:

- *Compliance:* we comply out of fear of retribution and disapproval, which can lead to a "see-saw" of control behavior and retraction

- *Control:* we try to manipulate others by instilling guilt in them, as in "You'll be sorry when I'm dead or when I run away from home"

- *Indifference:* we withdraw, which can lead to sullen, unresponsive behavior.

In all three strategies, we develop mechanisms to cope with outer rejection and the negative consequences of our coping mechanisms, such as fighting with siblings, meaningless activities such as "hanging out," and appearing as though nothing matters.

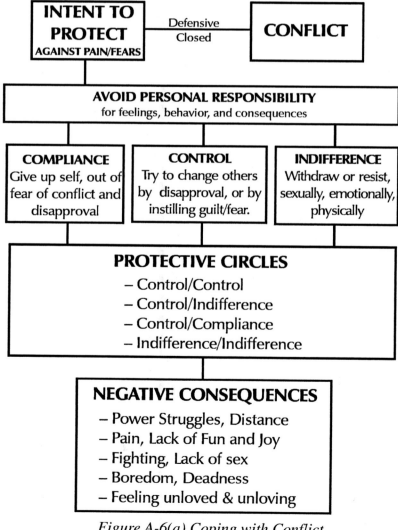

Figure A-6(a) Coping with Conflict

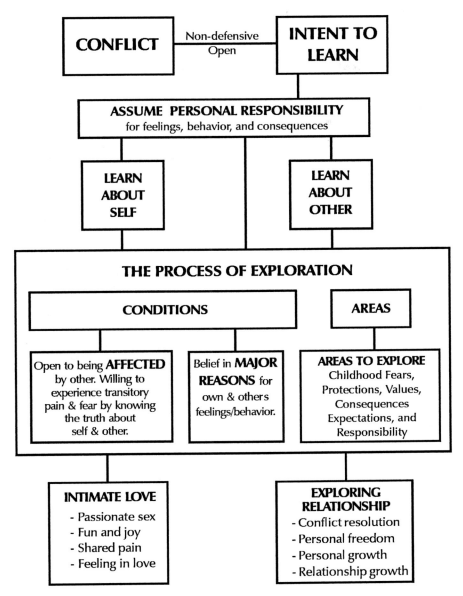

Figure A-6(b) Coping with Conflict

On the other hand, with self-esteem and self-worth intact, we are eager to learn about the world and how we can best interact with it. We take responsibility for our actions and their consequences, seeing life as a learning experience. This leads to three main areas of exploration:

- Ourselves and other people, accepting any transitory pain that may result as part of the rich tapestry life.

- Why we and others act and feel as we do, and seeking the reasons behind what happens.

- Areas such as childhood, fears, expectations, and personal responsibility.

This openness leads to being able to share love in intimate relationships, accepting them as arenas in which to resolve conflicts and explore personal freedom, the overarching goals being growth of self, other, and the relationship.

Appendix B

Body Map

As Figures B-1 and B-2 show, fear is stored on the left side of the body; anger on the right, with rejection along the spine. In fact, we have uncovered sixty individual locations for specific other emotional, dysfunctional programs.

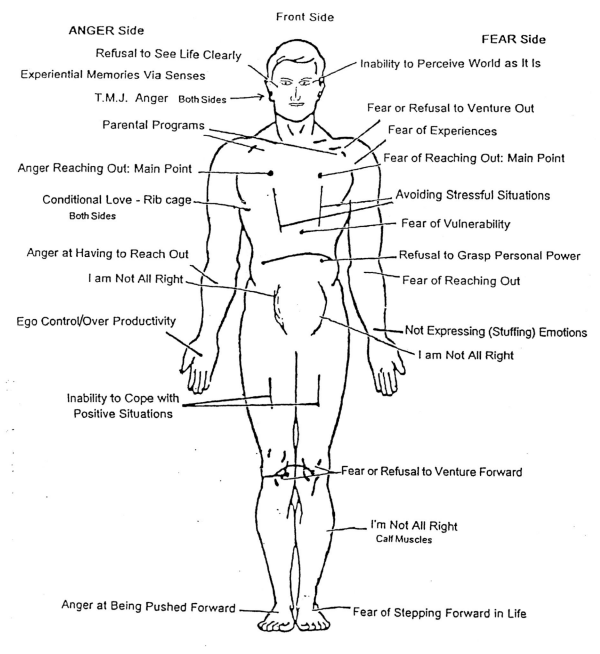

Figure B-1: Body Map Front

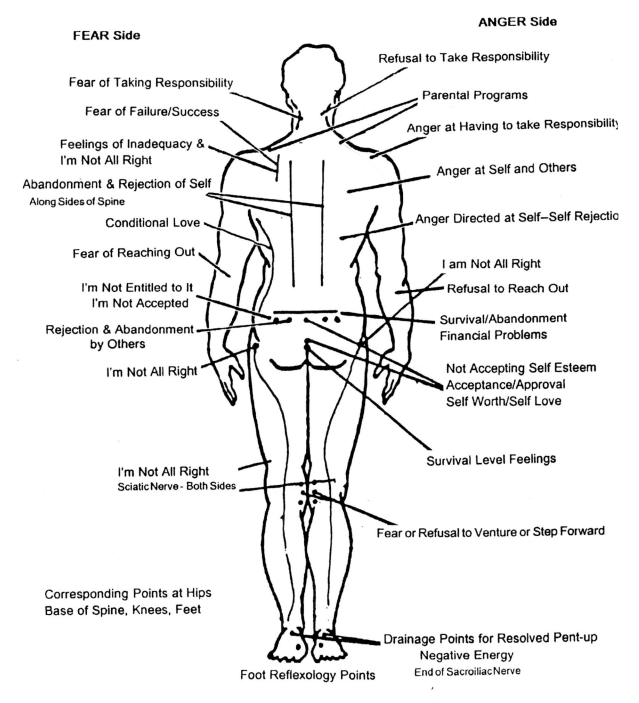

Figure B-2: Body Map Back

Appendix C

The StressBuster™

Disclaimer

The following description is of an experimental device intended for research in electronic medical experiments. We are not medical doctors or psychiatrists and we do not make any medical claims, nor can we prescribe or diagnose any ailment, illness or disease. Due to FDA regulations we cannot make any claims as to what these devices will accomplish.

The StressBuster Concept

Every living being in the universe has a particular frequency at which it resonates when in perfect health. Each component of that being's body also resonates at a particular frequency. If stress disrupts this frequency, the cellular structure of the organ or gland is weakened and will be subject to breakdown, disease or illness.

If you take two matched tuning forks and hit one, the other will vibrate at the same frequency. Your body does the same thing. When you are subject to forms of negative vibrations of stress, fear, anger, or resentment in your environment, you begin to identify with this hostile environment and your body begins to resonate with that vibration. If you go into flight or fight, your adrenals kick in, causing a strain on the immune and endocrine systems. A strong dose of adrenaline helps you handle the situation, so under stress, the adrenaline level in your body increases the energy available to cope with the perceived stress, danger, fear or anger. Under normal circumstances, your brain should signal that the stress is over with a shot of nor-adrenaline as an antidote so we can return to normal energy and frequency level. When the stress passes, we should return to 15 to 25 hertz.

If, however, you live in perpetual stress, survival, fear or confrontational conditions, your body frequency will rise to 1,000 or 2000 Hz and remain there. If the stress continues over time, the frequency may never return to a peaceful state.

The ideal 12 to 18 Hz but we have tested people with frequencies up to 2,000 Hz, which is over 100 times higher that it should be. The result will be that you begin to function solely on adrenaline as your body frequency continues to rise and maintain this stress level. Eventually, your body cannot return to the ideal frequency due to ongoing stress. We have found this to be the case with over 90% of the population.

The StressBuster unit emits a 15-foot diameter sphere of an Extremely Low Frequency (ELF) signal at the earth's resonance frequency, which is the ideal frequency for functioning of the body. The body/mind will identify with the frequency that has the strongest effect on it, so the StressBuster causes the body to identify with its low frequency by blocking out other frequencies that are stressful to the body. All of the brain chemicals such as interleukins, serotonin, interferon, etc., operate at the earth resonance of 12 to 15 Hz, and the immune system and the endocrine system work more effectively when there is no load on the adrenal glands.

The unit also emits a high frequency of 9.216 MHz, which creates a psychic "safe zone" that cannot be penetrated by lower astral entities.

Stress Buster Effect on the Body/Mind

Negative sensory input or negative thoughts and emotions cause the neuropeptides to have a similar effect on the immune and endocrine systems, which causes them to lower their ability to protect us against stress and illness. The electrical field around the body must be strong to ward off disease factors but, as the body frequency rises, the electrical and auric fields weaken. These fields are termed life force, chi, ki or prana, depending on the culture, and give us our overall strength, vitality and protection.

The following is a greatly simplified explanation of the theory behind the StressBuster. The information that causes the various parts of the body to operate is carried by the body's neurological network system. The brain serves as a "switching network center" that directs the information across the network to the appropriate parts of the body with electrical impulses through the meridian system and with chemicals known as neuropeptides and cytokinins. The Subconscious Mind is the repository for all programs and habit patterns. The other three levels of mind must work together and with the Subconscious Mind, or we will encounter malfunctions such as anger, fear, "I am not all right," rejection, abandonment, resentment, need for control, manipulation and relationship conflicts. These emotional programs then cause breakdowns in the physical body, leading to disease, illness and mental depression.

Each cell is a node in the network and receives its orders from the mind through the body's neurological system, carried by electrolytes, neuropeptides, and cytokinins. When operating properly, the cells maintain a delicate balance of chemicals, like the storage battery in your car. When they go out of balance or get run down, the electromagnetic fields breakdown. The result is as if "your batteries are run down." The body loses its ability to protect itself properly, and the brain/mind can no longer communicate with the cells, which become subject to attack by diseases, illness and outside forces. When the physical body is in harmony, it functions between 12 and 25 hertz. However, stress and emotional conflict cause the internal frequency to rise to 1,000 to 2,000 hertz. When this happens, the neuropeptides, electrolytes, and the neurological system cannot transmit electrical impulses through the body/mind network. The rise in frequency causes all body tissues from the skin to the organs and endocrine system to be subject to stress, breakdown and *accelerated aging.* This is the most damaging effect of increased stress and high frequency. The results are illness depression, chronic fatigue, emotional instability and life-threatening disease.

Metabolism is affected due to breakdown of the function of the endocrine glands, and absorption of the nutrition supplied to the body slows down. Feeling tired and depleted causes chronic fatigue and depression. As the internal frequency rises past 50 Hz, the "happy" brain chemicals shut down and the adrenals release more adrenaline to keep you functioning. The end result of overworked adrenal glands is adrenal insufficiency. They begin to produce less and less adrenaline, and when production drops to 30% or less of normal, fatigue sets in. Below 20%, you go into adrenal exhaustion, leading to Chronic Fatigue, Epstein Bar, which leads to clinical depression. (It is similar to low blood sugar caused by hypoglycemia which leads to diabetes but stress causes breakdown in all systems of the body.)

Many people run to the doctor and begin taking Prozac, Zantac, Zolov, Valium, Paxil or other mind-altering anti-depressant drugs. You can get addicted to these "feel good" drugs because they suppress the symptoms and trick the brain into believing the symptoms of total body malfunction are false messages.

The StressBuster's ELF signal encourages the body to operate at 12 to 25 hertz, where the adrenal glands can heal and resume their normal operating level. (For more information, see *Your Body Is Talking; Are you Listening?* by Art Martin $14.95 plus $3.00 shipping. Published by Personal Transformation Press, 800-655-3846.)

Operation of the StressBuster — Electronic Medical Research

The Stress Buster balances all the electrical, metabolic and electromagnetic systems that are dysfunctional, shutting out the disharmonious stress frequencies that the body tries to resonate with. It is operating at fifth dimensional energy. It strengthens all the systems of the body by bringing down the frequency to the optimum level for perfect health.

To be in balance, most devices, plants and animals have positive and negative energies that rotate clockwise and counterclockwise. This creates a balance in the electrical system. A few plants such as garlic, onion, and some herbs radiate a double positive field, hence their antibiotic, healing qualities. The StressBuster also radiates a double positive field which explains the response it creates.

For more than 200 years (since science has been able to measure it), the earth's most powerful resonant frequency, or Schuman Resonance Frequency, was 7.83 Hz. As of 2004, it has risen to between 12 and 14 Hz, and predictions are that it will stabilize at 13.5 Hz. Our original Harmonizers (the forerunner of the StressBuster) were built to emit 7.83 Hz, and we have increased the frequency along with the Schuman Resonance Frequency. The body will identify with this frequency and resonate with it, blocking out other interference.

How quickly will the body align to the StressBuster's frequency when it is within the 15-foot diameter bubble of the electromagnetic field? It may take up to three days depending on your body's frequency. Once you are inside the bubble, you will notice your body begin to slowdown and relax. When your body/mind resonates at this optimum level your body begins to heal.

With battery powered models, you may notice that the StressBuster needs to be recharged more often than once a week in the beginning because, if your body energy is low and you have been under considerable stress, the batteries will be drawn down faster as the unit interfaces and responds to your body energy level. Some users report having to charge the battery as often as every two days initially.

High Frequency Unit

The unit's high frequency emission of 9.216 MHz creates a psychic "safe zone" that cannot be penetrated by lower astral entities because earthbound spirits that try to attach to you cannot handle the frequency. It blocks the negative energy of psychic attacks that are sent by another person who may be sending their anger to you.

We chose 9.216 MHz after checking hundreds of frequencies. This is a universal frequency that will activate the body's healing modalities and repel anything or anybody who emits a negative energy.

Tesla Theory and Technology

We asked some electronic wizards and some physicists why we were getting a clear AC sine wave coupled with a scalar wave, without the circuitry to produce it. All they could say was, "You're dealing with hyper-dimensional physics and it's over our heads. We cannot explain it." Another said, "You are into Tesla and Einstein's realm, and we do not understand what you are doing." We are apparently producing an output that no one understands.

The StressBuster generates a bio-electrical magnetic field using electro-magnetic field technology developed by Nikola Tesla in the early 1900s. The coil-antenna produces a *scalar wave field* described as a longitudinal wave field that functions outside of three-dimensional space/time. Since it operates outside of space/time, it is unencumbered by the limitations of conventional physics. Scalar waves operate within the etheric field which surrounds the body.

In the summer of 2000 we changed builders. We are not working with self styled hackers anymore. Even our research consultants and engineers say, "As far as we can understand, it appears that we are in new territory that quantum physics has not yet explored. We cannot measure the scalar wave output as it exists outside conventional physical principles. But we *have* been able to measure the radio frequency carrier wave.

Background and History

With today's new computer technology and micro electronics, we have been able to reduce the size of the Tesla's original equipment by 90%. Over ten generations, we have refined the circuitry so that the unit is much more efficient and uses much less battery current. Originally, the unit used one 9-volt battery a week, which was quite expensive. We shifted to AA NiCad batteries but they had a charging memory, causing them to break down. We now use Nickel-Metal-Hydride batteries, which have no charging memory and last up to four years.

The first prototype did not have a very strong field, yet it worked so well that we continued our research. The prototype of the current generation had a triple-wound toroidal ferrite metal core coil that absorbed two thirds of the output. The current production unit has an 800 millivolt output and a bar antennae that puts out three times the power. There are no instruments available to measure a scalar field at this time, but we can pick up the radio frequency.

Testimonials

Disclaimer

Due to FDA regulations, we make no claims as to what the StressBuster will accomplish. We can only report what users have relayed to us. We check out the testimonials to find if we have multiple responses that verify the experiences people are having. Many claims have been made by users of the StressBuster, but we cannot recommend it for anything as we are not psychiatrists or doctors. We are not allowed by law to diagnose or prescribe. We believe these user reports to be accurate.

Here, we relay the experiences of those who have used the Harmonizer. For example, many people have reported that it pulled them out of depression in 5 – 14 days without any drugs, and many have ceased taking prescription antidepressants. Two psychiatrists validated this information from their experience.

In my case, I injured my foot with a chain saw, and the wound was not healing well but, as soon as I began using the new Harmonizer, my foot began to heal at an unprecedented rate. I could actually see it heal from one day to the next. The deep gash closed up and healed over in less than two weeks, and today has left only a faint red mark.

1. "It seems to bring programs to the surface that I had no awareness of. It's the best therapeutic tool I have come in contact with." *B.E., CA*

2. "I strapped the Harmonizer over a broken leg on the cast where the break was and the break healed four times faster than normal. The doctor was amazed that we could take the cast off in less than four weeks." *J.S., CA*

3. "Chronic Fatigue I'd suffered for years disappeared in less than a week." *J.C., Arizona*

4. "I am feeling general well being and able to handle stress more effectively. I'm not getting angry as quickly as in the past. One day, I left the Harmonizer at home and I noticed my stress level began to rise at work." *C.D., CA*

5. "Psychiatrists who have purchased the Harmonizer report that it works with depression very well since it reactivates the brain chemicals and supports the rebuilding of normal production of all the essential brain chemicals, allowing the adrenals to slow down and heal. As a result people seem to pull out of depression." *R.N., Virginia*

6. "I put the Harmonizer on a plant that was dying, and it revived in just one day." *T.K., CA*

7. "A burn totally disappeared in three days. This was apparently caused by the activation of the cellular restructuring." *J.T., CA*

8. "It apparently has caused my immune system to rebuild because I am recovering from a long term illness. It is feels great to get my stamina back." *W.B., NM*

9. "It activates programs in the mind that have been covered up for years. Apparently denial programs are forced to the surface." *H.M., CA*

10. "I am finding I have more energy and I sleep less now that the stress is relieved." *G.B., CO*

11. "I have been taking drugs for depression, and low thyroid and adrenal function. I continued to take the drugs until they ran out. I noticed that I was getting the same effect from the Harmonizer so I did not renew my prescriptions. That was three years ago and I have not had any depression since. And the new Harmonizer is even better. Thank you so much." *A.P., CA*

12. "I handed the unit to friend of mine and he dropped it immediately, saying he couldn't hold onto it. Once I cleared him of attached entities, he had no problem holding it." *J.O.E., CA*

13. "I had been to the doctor for my high blood pressure and he prescribed medication to control my blood pressure because it was 190 over 120. I checked it again a month later and it was still the same. I bought the Harmonizer and started carrying it with me all the time. Less than a month later, I was down to 120 over 70. The doctor could not understand how my blood pressure would come down to normal. 'That just does not happen to someone your age.' I cannot attribute it to anything other than the Harmonizer." *C.S., AZ*

14. "It is amazing. I felt burned out and the doctor said my adrenals were very low and wanted me to take drugs to build them back up. I told him I did not take drugs of any kind and would find another way. I started using the Harmonizer, and my adrenals recovered in three days. I do not feel as stressed out anymore. This is truly electronic medicine." *K.S., OR*

15. "I have had a umbilical hernia for 25 years, and have consistently refused surgery to repair it, instead doing exercises to strengthen the abdominal muscles so it would repair itself. It had been slowing getting smaller, but very slowly. I had the earlier version of the Harmonizer for four years and while it helped in many ways, it had no effect on the hernia. But with the new high frequency unit, in just three months the hernia has reduced to about one quarter of what it was last year." *A.M., CA*

16. "My husband had flu twice this winter and I usually get it from him and end up down for a week. This year, no flu or anything. I can only assume the Harmonizer protected me and kept my immune system up to par so I was not affected." *C.H., CA*

17. "For me, the Harmonizer is a miracle because I seem to go out of my body quite often and driving is very dangerous when this happens. I have been solidly in my body since I have been using the Harmonizer." *J.S., CA*

18.   "I have had serious immune system problems for years. It seems that I catch everything that comes along. The Harmonizer has upgraded my immune system to the point that I am now very seldom sick." *C.K., CA*

19.   "When I called to find out about the unit, I was willing to try anything as my blood pressure was 210 over 120 and I had lung congestion. My legs hurt so much I could not even walk around the grocery store. In five weeks my blood pressure dropped to 130 over 90 and still continues to fall. I have no lung congestion and I can drive trucks again. I have gone back to work full-time."

20.   "As a healer, I touch many clients in my work and would frequently have entities attaching to me from my clients. Today, I would not be without my 'boogie buster' because it protects me so well." *J.N., CA*

21.   "I have had low adrenal function almost all my life. Stress really takes me down to the point where I can't function. With the Harmonizer, I have recovered totally. I have not experienced any depression or lack of energy since I began using it." *C.K., CO*

22.   "Accelerated healing of burns has been amazing. I spilled boiling water on my face when I dropped a teakettle. The burn marks began clearing up in two weeks. In a month, they were almost gone except for redness on the skin. Today, there is no scarring and all the marks are gone." *M.K., AZ*

23.   "One of the most amazing results I have found from using the Harmonizer is that old burn scars and keeled scars are disappearing, some of which have been on my body for forty years. It is truly amazing." *H.M., CA*

24.   "After a motorcycle race, I suffered a serious third degree burn on my leg from an exposed exhaust pipe. The burn healed in less than one month, and in six weeks was just a dark spot. In the past, burns like this have taken six months to heal."

25.   "I have had panic attacks for fifteen years and cannot drive in traffic. Now I am able to drive anytime now without taking medicine." *K.W.H. PA*

26.   "I have been running at high speed, and my doctor told me to slow down. Being a workaholic, it was more stressful to push myself into slowing down which caused more problems The StressBuster did it, and I am back to normal."

These are only a few user reports. The most often reported effect is clearing depression lack of energy and being able to slow down. Others have reported much clearer mind and more vivid memory. People have experienced more clear and active meditations.

We have found that it accelerates the healing of cuts and wounds on the skin. It is apparently activating some cellular response as skin cuts seem to heal in one quarter of the normal time. The unit is activating/supporting the immune and endocrine system.

The only downside is that it brings up repressed emotional programs, and you *must* deal with the suppressed feelings and programs that are forced up.

People who have been harassed by earthbound spirit beings report being free of them as long as they keep the unit on them 24 hours a day. In this regard, we have found that the StressBuster far exceeds our expectations.

We hesitate to list more user reports because new users tend to expect certain results from the StressBuster. It is only an adjunct that works with your body, and although the StressBuster can be a catalyst for miracles, please do not put unrealistic expectations on it. Also, you must do your part in releasing your emotional trauma that it brings up. It can have a placebo effect, in that if you believe that it works, it works on almost anything.

Operating Instructions

Please read carefully before using the StressBuster. If you are unsure or do not understand these instructions, please contact the person who sold you the unit.

To charge the Portable StressBuster, plug the charging unit into a 120 VAC outlet (the black unit with the plug) and plug the metal jack into the charging socket on the StressBuster (the round socket next the light).

If you purchased the Stationary StressBuster, just plug it into a 120 VAC outlet in your house or office. Center it in the building so it has maximum effect throughout the area.

Important warning: Simply plug in the charger for four hours if it is fully discharged for the first time; 2 to 3 hours each week from then on. We are using Nickel Metal Hydride batteries now as they have no memory. You can charge them any time but it takes longer to charge them. If the red light goes out you will have to charge four hours. This is very important as we have had people return the unit with the complaint that battery was no good or would not charge. They had charged it with a cell phone charger of higher voltage or over charged the battery for more than eight hours.
Overnight Charges will not hurt the batteries but try to avoid long charge periods.

Be aware that the StressBuster can and will activate programs or activities in your body. It you feel agitated and do not want to use the unit, have someone clear you of attached spirit beings as directed in this Protocol Manual. We have had people return units, claiming they were making them sick. The StressBuster has only positive affects, but programs and attached spirit beings can make you sick or feel down. Once they are cleared, very seldom do we have any problems.

If you have feelings start to surface, try to find out what they are and release them if possible. Split personalities and sub-personalities can cause uneasiness if they feel that they are losing control over you.

It is best to keep the StressBuster within 5 feet of your body at all times 24/7 as it works as a bridge to balance your body. If you leave it somewhere, check yourself out to see it you have attached beings on you, as they see you as a target when you are using the StressBuster. After the first few days, things usually calm down and you will experience a sense of well being when your body slows down to operating at between 12 and 25 Hz.

Product Prices and Upgrades

1.   The price of the Portable 800 millivolt Body/Mind StressBuster 9.216 MHz unit is $297.00. The price in Canada varies depending on the current exchange rate, but will be between $400 and $475. Shipping within the USA is $5.00; shipping to Canada is about $10.00 US. Existing Harmonizers can be exchanged for an updated StressBuster for $25 to $100 depending what changes must be installed.

2.   A new Stationary StressBuster unit operates on 120V and has an overall balancing/clearing effect in offices, houses, seminar and workshop facilities. The challenge was to build a more powerful unit that would not interfere with SW or TV reception or be classified by the FCC as a portable radio station. Price $347.00.

3.   We are developing a unit that sweeps through 9 Hz to 12 MHz every three seconds to provide the benefits of the above four states of mind. The StressBuster acts as a bridge to allow you to experience these feeling states while working through the process of transformation. We do not have a date for release.

4.   We are working on a new 120 VAC unit that will combine both units plus a programming mode to hook up with a tape recorder or a CD player for use with music and voice tapes for reprogramming the mind. One unit will have an MP3 player built into it. It will also use piezo-electric discs similar to headphones to output information directly into the eighth cranial nerve, thus bypassing the Conscious Mind so it cannot tamper with or sabotage the input. In our tests, deaf people can hear the output from a microphone or from tapes played in the unit. People have reported learning a foreign language in as little as two weeks. A teacher reported that she was able to provide learning to disabled students that had not been possible in the past. Projected price is $795, depending on options. This will include some programming software.

The Stress Buster has a one year warranty and a lifetime guarantee. Return it to us and we will repair it. We will repair any malfunction in the unit at no charge. We charge for repairs for mishandling or damage caused by the user. If you are not pleased with your unit, we will refund your money anytime during the first year if the unit is returned in good condition. We will deduct a $25.00 restocking charge on used units, and the cost of repairing any damage or repairs.

To order the Body/Mind StressBuster, call or write:

Energy Medicine Institute
8300 Rock Springs Rd.
Penryn, CA 95663
FAX: 916- 663-0134
Toll-free order line: 800- 655-3846
E-mail: artmartin@mindspring.com
WebSites: www.medicalelectronics.us
www.stressbuster.org

Appendix D

Glossary

This book uses terms that are not in common usage today. This glossary will help in understanding them.

A Course In Miracles: a set of three books that describes how we can change our view of forgiveness and love, and achieve peace and happiness through understanding who we are in relation to the Holy Spirit. The teacher's manual tells us that we are all students and teachers at all times in our life. The lesson manual shows us how to change our concept of who we are each day.

Addiction: compulsion or obsession about a situation or a substance that will cover up, meet a need or avoid a situation. The paradox: getting too much of what you do not need to satisfy an emotional imbalance in life.

Ascension: an evolutionary process of becoming a light being through releasing all the emotions and control sub-personalities that drive our life. Being able to reclaim our personal power and become a "no limit" person. The final result is getting off the cycle of return (reincarnation).

Back-up files: each day, the mind backs up all its files just as you would with a computer to save and protect your files.

Clairvoyant, Clairaudient: using our sixth senses to see and hear beyond normal restrictions of sight and hearing.

Collective Mind: a collection of information from all areas of the universe. Could be also described as the Akashia.

Conscious Rational Mind: the mind that we use to input information and data to the Subconscious Mind's files.

Cosmic phone line: a connection into the higher forces with no discernible source.

Dark Forces: beings from the astral plane, commonly described as demons, devil, satanic or Luciferian beings.

Denial: the first level of locking up programs so you do not have to deal with them. They can be located in any of the four minds.

Denial-of-denial: when an incident is too traumatic to deal with, we lock it up in denial-of-denial so that we cannot access it at all. However, it can affect our mental state even though we are unaware of it.

Divination: gaining answers using any form of an instrument, such as dowsing, pendulums, or oracles.

Ego or File Manager: the aspect of our mind that files the records in and retrieves information from the Subconscious Mind's data files. (I prefer the term *Middle Self.*)

Grace: that which is accorded to us to clear karma. When we acknowledge we have learned the lesson from a karmic experience, contract, or agreement, we can claim Grace and the Lords of Karma will delete the lesson from our Akashic Record.

GOD: (uppercase) the GOD Source or Presence of GOD.

God: (lowercase) the Christian or religious reference to God.

Holographic Mind: the soul level of mind that is in direct contact with Higher Self. It has access to all the records in the mind and Akashic. Will provide help when you request it. The all-knowing mind.

Karma: contracts that are created by dishonest, unethical or out-of-integrity behavior. If you kill someone even if in the line of duty, a karmic agreement is created. If you harm someone in anyway, you create a karmic contract.

Kinesiology: a form of divination that uses the various muscles of the body to answer questions. When accessing the mind through muscle testing for answers, the neuromotor responses are indicated through either strong or weak muscular response depending on how you assign Yes or No.

Lords of Karma: beings from the spiritual plane that reside with the GOD Source and help us file our flight for each life. They maintain the Akashic Record.

Love: a manifestation of actions and feelings that support growth, happiness, joy, peace of mind and acceptance.

Middle Self: the middle mind made up of the Conscious Mind, Instinctual Mind and Inner Middle Self. All the sub-personalities are installed in the Middle Self files. Quite often, it is misidentified as Ego because it exhibits the qualities that people generally ascribe to Ego.

Mystery School: an esoteric school that has existed for thousands of years. Many teachers who have been given the information by GOD Source have carried the tradition on. The teachers are chosen by the White Brotherhood and GOD Source. Many self-proclaimed teachers have set up mystery schools, calling for discernment as to who are the true teachers.

Psychoneuroimmunolgy: a new concept developed by Robert Adler, a faculty member of the Rochester Medical School, where he is now Director of the Department of Psychoneuroimmunology Research. The basic concept is that mental states control the distribution and production of chemicals that communicate with the various systems within the mind/body. They control the immune and endocrine functions, which in turn control heath and wellness.

Quickening: the increase in planetary vibration caused by the shift in energy on the planet.

Spiritual Practice: a discipline one follows in an effort to develop spirituality.

Spiritual Journey: the path to transformation that entails learning many lessons in letting go of limitations, emotions and karma.

Spirituality: the result of learning the lessons on the path; the process of becoming a person who functions with honesty, ethics and integrity.

Universal Laws: the laws that govern the universe. The specific laws are set up to control interactions and apply to all planetary systems and star groups. (On this planet, we do not seem to acknowledge this simple form of law.)

About The Author

In today's world, the issue of credibility often comes up. How many degrees do you have? What colleges did you attend? Who did you study with? Who were your teachers? How do you know this works?

When I needed outside validation and acceptance, those were valid questions. Now I do not consider them valid, nor do I care if others reject me because I don't have the credibility they seek. What I learned in college has no relevance to what I do now in my practice. What I know is far more important than my background. Therefore, I am not interested in listing all my credentials.

Neuro/Cellular Repatterning is a process that was developed by myself and three people who worked with me during the research period: Dr. James Dorabiala, Mike Hammer and Bernard Eckes. And new information still pours in even today. This is basically a self-taught process, and everyone who worked with us over the last 20 years are our students and our teachers.

What *is* relevant is that we be open to new ideas. I will attend others' workshops and experience their treatments. Healing is an open-ended and ongoing process in which we need to be open to new ideas. The "sacred cow" syndrome is out-dated and does not work for me.

Someone once attacked me with, "You think you have the whole pie, don't you? You believe that nobody can match up to you."

My response was, " I don't think I have the whole pie, but based on the success of the last 20 years, maybe I have a few more pieces than some other practitioners."

Art was born into a family where his father wanted a child and his mother did not. As an only child, he did not have any sibling interaction, so his only contacts were at school. His dysfunctional family laid down many problems, which he has come a long way in clearing, thanks to discovery of the process he developed—Neuro/Cellular Repatterning—and the people who worked with him over the years.

In 1963, he quit college after five years feeling frustrated with the educational system. He dabbled in real estate, but found that it was not his calling. In 1965, he married Susie, his partner ever since. Their sons, Ross and Ryan, were born in 1971 and 1976.

Very few people in the field of therapy work seem to be able to stay in a relationship due to the fact they do not want to deal with their own issues. Art was committed to find himself and went on a path to do so. He stabilized his own relationship by working out his issues.

In 1968, he and Susie found themselves in St. Helena, CA, rebuilding an abandoned winery. To clear the land to plant grapes, Art became a logger. To support his family while the winery was being rehabilitated, he hired out his D8 Caterpillar tractor for land-clearing and vineyard preparation. After seven years, the big money interests were pushing grape prices below what was economically viable for a small winery to stay in business, so he sold the winery.

His next venture was a restaurant which he built himself, but found that the restaurant field is one of the most demanding there are. Despite instant financial success, he sold the restaurant after four months and moved on. However, Art met his first teacher at the restaurant, someone who planted a seed of doubt about his life path. At the time, Art was trying to find himself and was studying extensively and attending self-improvement seminars. After closing time, they would spend many hours talking about their paths.

In 1978, the buyers of the restaurant went bankrupt, so their payments stopped. Art had to return to work and his quest was disrupted. Fortunately, Susie was working full-time, but in 1980, she was laid off and Art, who had a green thumb, worked as a gardener at a senior citizens' complex. Having closely studied the Findhorn community, he took the opportunity to apply what he had learned about the earth spirits. He found, from the plants themselves, that the landscape architect had put many of them in the wrong place. Over the next year, he transformed the barren grounds into magnificent flower gardens, and even built a passive solar greenhouse to grow flowers year around.

By 1982, his healing practice was established so he quit the gardener job and concentrated on researching healing practices.

Art soon found that Santa Rosa, CA did not support the type of work he was doing, and when Joshua Stone invited him to go to Los Angeles to give readings to clients, he jumped at the opportunity. He and Joshua found they worked well together as a team, and Art was able to provide a unique and valuable service to many therapists. However, the traveling almost broke up his family, so they moved to Sacramento, CA, and opened a bookstore and metaphysical center.

While Art received considerable support for this venture, he didn't anticipate that few people had the money to support it financially. Having invested all the family's savings, and refinanced their house, all went well for almost three years until he took on partners in order to expand. However, his partners did not understand the law of cause and effect, and when they embezzled $28,000, the business went under.

Knowing that "What goes around comes around," Art managed to accept what had happened, forgive them and get on with his life. However, trying to understand the lesson in this was hard to accomplish. When you are angry at losing your life savings and 20 years of hard work, the clarity and acceptance that he had set it all up came slowly. Even though he knew this at one level, it was a hard lesson to learn. The lesson was that while he received much verbal validation from those who supported the center, he was paying over half its operational costs.

The failure was a mixed blessing. It put him on a new path, one in which he traveled and spread the word of his work, and really had to get down to business. He did finally recover, even though they lost their house and one of their cars.

Looking back, Art recognizes the many great strides forward that he has made. Today, he travels extensively giving lectures, seminars and workshops on a variety of subjects. He also has a circuit of cities that he visits regularly for individual sessions.

He has set up a publishing company to promote his books (see list in the front of this book), and they are available through the Wellness Institute. Many of them will be in bookstores in 1999.

He can be reached at 1 800 OK LET GO (655-3846)

Printed in the United States
66382LVS00006B/100